Leading and *Managing*

A Differentiated Classroom

ASCD MEMBER BOOK

Many ASCD members received this book as a
member benefit upon its initial release.

Learn more at: **www.ascd.org/memberbooks**

SUSTAINABLE
FORESTRY
INITIATIVE

Certified Fiber Sourcing
www.sfiprogram.org

Leading and Managing

A Differentiated Classroom

Carol Ann Tomlinson
Marcia B. Imbeau

Alexandria, Virginia USA

ASCD®

1703 N. Beauregard St. • Alexandria, VA 22311 1714 USA
Phone: 800-933-2723 or 703-578-9600 • Fax: 703-575-5400
Website: www.ascd.org • E-mail: member@ascd.org
Author guidelines: www.ascd.org/write

Gene R. Carter, *Executive Director*; Judy Zimny, *Chief Program Development Officer*; Nancy Modrak, *Publisher*; Scott Willis, *Director, Book Acquisitions & Development*; Julie Houtz, *Director, Book Editing & Production*; Jamie Greene, *Editor*; Catherine Guyer, *Senior Graphic Designer*; Mike Kalyan, *Production Manager*; Sarah Plumb, *Production Specialist*

Printed in the United States of America. Cover art © 2010 by ASCD. ASCD publications present a variety of viewpoints. The views expressed or implied in this book should not be interpreted as official positions of the Association.

All web links in this book are correct as of the publication date below but may have become inactive or otherwise modified since that time. If you notice a deactivated or changed link, please e-mail books@ascd.org with the words "Link Update" in the subject line. In your message, please specify the web link, the book title, and the page number on which the link appears.

Figure 2.1 on page 32 is used with permission from *Differentiation and the Brain: How Neuroscience Supports the Learner-Friendly Classroom* by David A. Sousa and Carol Ann Tomlinson. Solution Tree Press, 555 North Morton Street, Bloomington, IN 47404, 800.733.6786. All rights reserved. Solution Tree is a leading provider of educational strategies and tools that improve staff and student performance. Visit solution-tree.com for more information.

ASCD Member Book, No. FY11-2 (Nov 2010, PSI+). ASCD Member Books mail to Premium (P), Select (S), and Institutional Plus (I+) members on this schedule: Jan., PSI+; Feb., P; Apr., PSI+; May, P; July, PSI+; Aug., P; Sept., PSI+; Nov., PSI+; Dec., P. Select membership was formerly known as Comprehensive membership.

PAPERBACK ISBN: 978-1-4166-1074-8   ASCD product #108011
Also available as an e-book (see Books in Print for the ISBNs).

Quantity discounts for the paperback edition only: 10–49 copies, 10%; 50+ copies, 15%; for 1,000 or more copies, call 800-933-2723, ext. 5634, or 703-575-5634. For desk copies: member@ascd.org.

Library of Congress Cataloging-in-Publication Data

Tomlinson, Carol A.
Leading and managing a differentiated classroom / Carol Ann Tomlinson & Marcia B. Imbeau.
    p. cm.
   Includes bibliographical references and index.
   ISBN 978-1-4166-1074-8 (pbk. : alk. paper) 1. Individualized instruction—United States. 2. Inclusive education—United States. 3. Classroom management—United States. I. Imbeau, Marcia B. II. Title.
   LB1031.T67 2011
   371.39'4—dc22   2010027600

20 19 18 17 16 15 14 13 12 11 10   1 2 3 4 5 6 7 8 9 10 11 12

For the teachers who didn't give up on us,
whose aspirations helped us find something better in ourselves than we had seen before,
who first helped us find ourselves,
and then, by example and experience, taught us the enlivening power of learning.
And to the people who from the beginning until now
whose steady love compels us each day to ask the question as we enter classrooms,
"Which person in this place is not in need
of the same sense of possibility they have given us?"

Leading and Managing a Differentiated Classroom

Preface

Far away there in the sunshine are my highest aspirations. I may not reach them, but I can look up and see their beauty, believe in them, and try to follow where they lead.

—Louisa May Alcott

I couldn't tell you in much detail about my sixth year of teaching, or my tenth, or any other specific year in the 21 years I spent in high school, preschool, and middle school classrooms except my first and fourth years. There are memories from each of the years I taught in public school that will always reside in me, of course, but no other particular years exist in my mind with the sharp detail of those two. It was in those two years that I established my compass as a teacher.

During my teenage years, I vowed never to be a teacher. My mother was a teacher (and immensely proud of her work), which was fine with me—until she and I ended up in the same school during my 6th grade year. It was a hard year for me. Not only was I entering adolescence with an impressive case of self-consciousness, but I was attending a new school in a new town. We had just moved away from the town where I'd spent the entire 11 years of my life to a new city where, on principle, I didn't *want* to like anything. My mom was a devoted mother. My teacher that year was one of the best I ever had. Nonetheless, it was clear to me that my mother came home with knowledge of things I had said or done during the day. I felt spied on, and that nourished my self-consciousness. With the lack of logic that is adolescence, I concluded that I did not want to be one of those "spy people" who watched kids and told on them. (Forget that my teacher was supportive and kind and tried to make my life better; she was a spy and I was the one spied upon.)

So, I declared, I would do anything but teach when I grew up. I persisted with that declaration at appropriate points in the 10 years that followed—including when my mother explained that I should take education courses in college, "just in case."

I explained with disdain that it was pointless for me to take education courses. Perhaps, I said, she didn't recall that I had long declared I would never, under any circumstances, teach. She told me she would support any college major I chose, as long as I took enough education courses on the side to become certified, "just in case."

I explained with louder disdain that I was a young adult who had earned the right to make her own decisions. She explained with remarkable calmness that she was paying the bill for my college tuition. I took the education courses, found them pointless, and renewed my vow often and vociferously that I would never, ever, under any circumstances be a teacher.

A Career Begins

I got my first job as a teacher in late October during my second year out of school. I was working as an advertising manager for a university press and had discovered another job that I disliked. Introvert that I was, I still couldn't warm up to a job that called on me to sit alone in a small room, day after day working with esoteric copy for esoteric books. Then, at lunch one day in October, I found a newspaper ad for a teaching job. Magically, it sounded like a wonderful opportunity.

I took the afternoon off, went for the interview, was hired, adjusted on the spot to my new title of high school English and history teacher, and resigned from the university press. The weekend between my conversion and reality, I experienced the excited apprehension that probably typifies entry into the teaching profession.

On Monday, I arrived at my new K–12 school, which was about an hour and 15 minutes from my house. It was in an area that gave sharp definition to the word *rural*. The little town had a name, a post office, a flue shop (tobacco-curing supplies), and an auto body shop. The post office closed shortly after I arrived because it had too little business. The flue shop fared well enough because of the local tobacco growers. The body shop thrived because of its location near a railroad track where the road dipped about 12 inches with no warning.

The principal of the school where I was about to begin (what I assumed would be a one-year career) seldom came to school during the early part of the day. He was shy and, I think, quite afraid of the older students. The assistant principal took me to my new classroom as the day began and announced to the very small, elderly teacher in the classroom that he was fired. He had been the teacher for the first six weeks of school, and because he commuted with a carpool, he had no way to go home until the end of the day. He was understandably angry and told me that, since he was no longer employed, I should see what I could do with the class. Despite befuddled terror and massive shyness, I found enough voice to say to him that I'd been promised a day to observe and get textbooks before I started teaching, and so I believed it would be better if I just sat in the back of the room.

For the rest of the day, I watched from the rear of my first classroom as high school girls giggled and chatted and boys crawled in and out of the first floor window and tried (unsuccessfully) to set a large freestanding bulletin board on fire. As I watched, two thoughts played in an endless loop in my mind: "What am I going to do with this chaos tomorrow?" and "I don't think I need a job this badly."

Recall that, as a student, I found my education classes to be without merit. Whether that was the result of the classes themselves or the result of my attitude about taking them, the reality of my new situation was that I had no idea how to teach, which seemed less important than my overriding realization that I had not the first clue about how to "manage" the high school students who were clearly in need of "being managed." At that point, my sole ambition as a teacher had to do with keeping the kids in their seats.

In my overwrought condition, I arrived at my very first lesson plan at 3:42 a.m. on Tuesday morning. It was a truly stupid plan that seemed completely acceptable at the time. I would have the students complete a crossword puzzle with me. The intent of the plan was twofold. First, it would buy me a day to figure out what the students knew and didn't know about American literature and world history— the two subjects, it turns out, I had been hired to teach. Second, it would let me establish myself as someone who gave clear and effective directions to students so we would have order in the classroom—in other words, the kids would stay in their seats.

The crossword puzzle, however, had nothing to do with the either literature or history. Its qualification for my first lesson plan was that it was the only crossword puzzle I could find in the middle of the night. It provided no window at all into my students' knowledge of our content, and the idea students would follow directions simply because I gave them was beyond naïve.

My first day as a teacher should have been a cosmic disaster. Instead, it taught me the first of many lessons I learned that year that have continued to serve me well ever since.

Classroom Management 101, Lesson 1

It turns out that my students were from a universe largely unrelated to the one where I grew up. Most of them had never left the insular area where they were born. None of them had college-educated parents, and few of them had any aspirations for a career—or even a job. They had no sense of a wider world. Old suspicions and animosities permeated their community. Yet they were happy, thoughtful, full of a wisdom the likes of which I had never encountered, and wide open to new possibilities despite the fact that they were pretty sure I was from an alien planet. "Outsiders" didn't show up very often in their world.

I got my students' attention when I asked them to take assigned seats as they entered the room. They were surprised because they were unaccustomed to assigned seats, and for a moment, they were caught off guard. Things looked promising. Then I passed out the crossword puzzles, intending to ask students to work in pairs on a specified portion of the puzzle. After a while, we would come together to check the portion of the work they had completed and then proceed in stages—work in pairs, come together, check work, go back to the pairs. It was a plan for the choreography of a teacher giving directions and students following them.

There was a problem with my plan. Not a single one of my 10th grade students, I quickly realized, had ever seen a crossword puzzle. They turned the purple ditto sheets in their hands as if they were seeking some sort of physical orientation to the task. When I realized this, I adjusted my plans accordingly. I'd just give directions to the class as a whole, and we'd figure out the puzzle together. After all, answers to the crossword puzzle were secondary. What mattered was that I gave good directions and that the students followed them.

I hit another more serious roadblock when I read the first clue to the students. It said, "Our country, abbr." The puzzle had three blank boxes for the answer. In the moment that followed, my students' faces and a few verbal hints revealed that (1) no one knew what the clues had to do with the boxes, (2) there might have been some confusion about "across" vs. "down," (3) no one knew what an abbreviation was (yielding a serious problem with the abbreviation of *abbreviation*), and, most significantly, (4) not a single student knew the name of our country. Once I shared with them the information necessary to address problem 4, after sequences of guesses from students, we encountered a fifth problem—a country whose name has four parts (United States of America) and only three boxes to enter the abbreviation. In all five of my classes that day, the bell rang as I announced that our country was called the United States of America and the abbreviation for that name was USA. It took an entire class, but we were finally ready to enter an answer for clue 1 across.

At the end of the day, I was exhausted, delighted with the extreme orderliness of my classes, and devoid of ideas about what I should do on Wednesday. I was also too tired and too new to understand what I had learned that day, but my first principle of classroom management eventually became clear. When students are engaged, they have no motivation to misbehave. My students were models of deportment on that day not because I stood in front of them and gave directions, of course, but because I had happened onto a task (albeit a vacuous one) that intrigued them.

Classroom Management 101, Lesson 2

My education as a teacher continued throughout the year, with a second pivotal lesson about classroom management coming about two weeks later. In the interim, we had good moments and bad. Although I was trying hard, I truly didn't know what I was doing. I couldn't steer a steady course because I didn't yet know why some things worked and others didn't.

It was to my advantage that I was a novelty for the students—a very tall teacher from the outside world who continued to do the unexpected in a school where nearly all the faculty were "lifers" in the community. We still used seating charts, and I was still big on making sure I gave clear directions, which I was attempting to do on the following Monday, when, about 10 minutes after the tardy bell, a formidable girl entered the classroom by slamming the door against the wall and standing with her hands on her hips and an "I dare you to mess with me" look on her face.

The class (which had been listening to the directions for another of my unorthodox assignments) looked at her wide-eyed, signaling that they knew her and were not about to mess with her. That flipped a switch in my head, and I recalled that a student had been absent from first period since I arrived. I smiled at the student and greeted her. "I bet you're Estralita," I said. "I'm Carol Tomlinson, and I'm the new teacher for this class. Everyone has an assigned seat now and yours is right up here." I pointed to a vacant seat in the front row. She stared for another second or two, emitted a sound that can only be described as a snort, and headed for the back of the room.

What happened next could have gone in a very different direction. I smiled at Estralita again broadly and said, "We've missed you, Estralita. I'm glad you're back. Now get your sorry self in your assigned seat up here so you can work with us." Immediately, I launched into the directions again. The class inhaled collectively. Her eyes flashed. She looked puzzled because no one was misbehaving. She pivoted and then stalked to the front of the room, threw her books on the floor, and sat like an angry bull for the rest of the class. I smiled at her again as the period ended and told her I was looking forward to getting to know her. She snorted.

The next day, Estralita was again absent as class began, but a rerun of the day before played out when the door bashed against the wall about 10 minutes into class. As Estralita filled the doorway with both her body and presence, I smiled at her and said, "I'm so glad you came today; I was afraid you were absent." The class froze. She stared. Then, with a harrumph, she launched toward the back of the class. Once again, I said, "Estralita, get your sorry self in your assigned seat" and continued without a pause with what I had been saying. Once again, she surveyed the territory, noticed that the class was with me, stalked to the front of the room, and deposited herself in the empty seat that was assigned to her.

We continued our ballet of the absurd for four days. On Friday, our dance began again. Ten minutes into class, door slamming, Estralita filling the doorway and the classroom with her bulk and anger, teacher smiling and greeting her, pregnant pause, Estralita heading toward the back of the classroom. All the moves were predictable now, except the one that would end the dance.

As she propelled herself to the rear of the room, I began my now well-rehearsed response, "Estralita. . . ." She interrupted, "I know. I gotta get my sorry self in my assigned seat." And she did. At the time, I didn't realize that something important had happened. I just plowed ahead. In that moment, though, Estralita decided to join us. She made the choice to be a member of the class, rather than a combatant.

Again, I didn't know for several months the importance of Estralita's decision in my survival as a teacher, and it was good that I didn't. It would have undone my fragile sense of "control." Much later in the year, I learned that Estralita had been suspended from school because she had argued with the teacher I replaced and literally knocked him unconscious to the floor. She was absent for my first week because that was the term of her expulsion. I was hired not because I had great credentials in English (and clearly not because I knew history), but rather because I was physically large enough to confront Estralita.

In the end, however, it was not my size that won the day with Estralita. It was her sense that I was somehow accepting of her—that I somehow felt she belonged in the class and that there was a place for her there. In time, I came to understand my second lesson of classroom management: If students understood that I saw them as worthwhile people with significant potential, it opened doors to learning.

My "get your sorry self in your assigned seat" comment could be seen as challenging or sarcastic. It was, however, delivered with a sincere smile and a sense of endearment. She saw in my face and heard in my tone that something was different in the classroom. For the first time she could remember, someone seemed to greet her with positive expectations. It took weeks, if not months, for her to truly begin trusting me, but from our first encounter, she felt invited. That was enough to buy us both some time—and to teach me once again that my penchant for directions was not enough to make me an effective "classroom manager."

Classroom Management 101, Lesson 3

I learned many lessons about life and "managing" a classroom during the remainder of my first year as a high school teacher. I learned how to pace lessons, how to organize materials, how to start and stop class with purpose, and how to shift gears if something wasn't going well, to name just a few. It was hard to leave Estralita and her peers when the year ended and I moved to another state. I still think about them nearly four decades later.

My second year as a teacher was spent as director of and teacher in a preschool with a very international population in a metropolitan area. Once again, I had no idea what I was doing. Once again, I learned important lessons through instinct, error, and luck. Once again, my students taught me more than I was prepared to teach them.

It was in my third setting, this time in a district where I would teach for 20 years, that my third career-shaping lesson about "managing" a classroom presented itself.

As was the case with my first two schools, the student population pushed on the perimeter of my experiences. In this school, we had a bimodal population. In my 7th grade language arts classes, nearly 50 percent of students read four or more years below grade level, and nearly 50 percent of students read four or more years above grade level. There were almost no "middle" students.

At this point in my development, I was excited to see a new school year begin. I finally believed I was a teacher. The students had not devoured me in terms of "classroom management" during my initial years, and now I even had a clear sense of my curriculum. I had a thick teacher's guide I developed with some of my colleagues during the summer after my first year in the school. Gone were the days of staying up late on Monday to figure out what to teach on Tuesday and then staying up late on Tuesday to figure out what to teach on Wednesday. Thanks to this guide, I not only knew on Monday what I should teach on Tuesday, but I knew in September what I would be teaching in May. With confidence that I was in control of the students and curriculum, I was jazzed when the beginning of my fourth year in the classroom rolled around.

My world shifted rapidly when I met Golden. He was 15 when he came up to me in the hall between classes. Two weeks into the year, he was about to join my 12-year-old 7th graders in second period. He approached me during a class change and whispered something I could not hear. The hall resonated with student talk. He was short and I was tall. He spoke with his hand over his mouth. After three tries, I said to him, "I'm so sorry, but it's really noisy and I just can't hear what you're saying. Let's try this once more. I'll bend down so I'm closer to you so I can hear better. You keep your hand down this time. I want to hear what you're trying to tell me."

What he was saying to me was "I can't read," and he was telling me the truth. He was three years too old for 7th grade, and he did not know the whole alphabet. For my part, I didn't know how to teach reading, but I did know that his "confession" was an act of courage and trust, and there was no way I could let him down.

In that flash of time in the hallway, a rush of questions filled my mind—and they have driven my work ever sense. How do I teach reading when I've never been trained for that? How do I make this boy a respected member of the class when he can neither read nor write? Do I seat him near someone who is really smart and let that student help him? Do I try to hide the fact that he is so far behind? What materials will I use with him? How can I find time to work with him on the things he needs? How in the world will I handle report cards in a way that is not demoralizing? Perhaps my most frightening realization was that the curriculum notebook I was sure would pave the way to my success as a teacher was suddenly an encumbrance—at least in my work with Golden.

For months, I obsessed about Golden as I tried to answer these questions (and others) that wouldn't leave me alone. We made some progress, and I began to figure out a rhythm for working with him in spite of 35 other students in the room. His needs were very different than what the curriculum anticipated, so I began to create a different curriculum for him that was embedded within the wider curriculum I had to teach everyone.

Then I thought about Jonathan. He had been in class all year. He was a good kid, he was smart and funny, and he made good grades. One day in the early spring, though, I really saw him for the first time. I was teaching a lesson on symbols in literature—a tricky topic for 7th graders who are often still a bit concrete in their thinking. I was proud of my concept attainment lesson on the topic. It was well planned, and the kids couldn't have responded better. After an examination of objects and photos of objects, I felt comfortable that the students were ready to name the concept we were pursuing—in this case, symbols. They offered their labels with only modest hesitation. Most students thought the objects should be called "signs." One suggested "trademarks." After a long silence, one final student proposed that we call them "logos."

When it was clear that no one else had any options to offer and silence overtook the class, many students literally looked across the room to Jonathan. In compliance with their silent signal to save the teacher, he raised his hand, sighed, and said with audible weariness, "They're symbols." The students were satisfied to know that if Jonathan had spoken, the right answer was on the table. I was pleased because the awkward silence ended.

We then tried to define the things we'd been happily investigating. The task was too ambiguous—too risky—for most students. I didn't know about Think-Pair-Share or reflective journals or even wait time, and so the silence wrapped around us again. Once more, students looked to Jonathan, and once again, he raised his hand. "What do you think a symbol is?" I asked him gratefully. Once again he sighed and, without pause, provided the definition he carried in his head—had carried in his head for goodness knows how many years. "A symbol," he said, "is an abstract representation of a concrete entity."

In that moment, I understood my third principle of classroom management: The classroom can't work for anybody until it works for everybody!

The problem wasn't that Golden had one set of needs and everyone else had another. The problem was that I had a room full of students with widely differing needs. I couldn't make the classroom work for Golden as well as it needed to because I was trying to "fit him in" around the edges of "the real" agenda. At that point, I saw clearly that my magical curriculum guide failed Jonathan as surely as it failed Golden. I somehow had to learn to plan a classroom where flexibility provided opportunity for everyone.

In other words, I understood at that moment that an effective teacher is not someone who just teaches content. He or she is someone who teaches content to human beings, and the classroom has to work in such a way that each individual in it has a legitimate opportunity to grow as much as possible from his or her starting point.

I realized, then, that classroom management is the process of figuring out how to set up and orchestrate a classroom in which students sometimes work as a whole group, as small groups, and as individuals. The goal would be to have everyone work not only on things they all need to do in common but also on things that were of particular importance for their own individual growth.

This insight indicated considerable growth in me as a teacher. I had progressed from defining "classroom management" as (1) keeping kids in their seats, to (2) giving good directions, to (3) being rooted in engaging curriculum, to (4) stemming from genuine respect for each student, and, finally, to (5) making room for individual and group needs. Each new realization built upon and broadened my understanding of what it meant to be a teacher. Each year in the classroom, each class and each student were catalysts for my continuing growth in understanding and practice.

In time, I came to be a little uncomfortable with the term "classroom *management.*" I don't like being *managed* myself, and I realized that I respond much better to being *led.* Ultimately, I understood that a part of my role was leading students and managing the details and mechanics of the classroom. Therefore, I began to think about the distinction between being a leader in and a manager of the classroom. Still later, I came to understand the interdependence of learning environment, curriculum, assessment, and instruction. I understood more clearly the ways in which classroom leadership and management were part of one system and how they could enable me to use all of the classroom elements to reach each of my students.

Throughout my career, I learned to think about time, space, materials, groups, and strategies in ways that balanced content requirements and the needs of young learners. I happened upon and invented ways to make the classroom more efficient for me and more effective for my students. Likewise, I happened upon and invented ideas that appropriately met a quick demise. This book reflects much of that learning, both things worth considering and things to avoid.

The book that follows is presented in two parts. The first part focuses on what it means for a teacher to effectively *lead* a differentiated classroom. The second part focuses on the mechanics of *managing* a differentiated classroom. In practice, of course, teachers must think about both elements at once. It's likely, however, that looking at the roles of leader and manager separately clarifies two complementary but distinct lines of thinking that contribute to teacher and student success.

My coauthor for this book is Marcia Imbeau, a good friend, colleague, and stellar mentor for novice teachers. Her own teaching experience is as rooted in the elementary classroom as mine is rooted in the secondary classroom. We both know that the principles of managing or leading an effectively differentiated classroom are the same across grades and subjects, but we also know that teachers want and need to see illustrations that match their teaching assignments. We hope to provide authentic and tested examples of the principles at work in varied grade levels and in varied subjects.

In addition, we both know there is no recipe for effective leadership and management in a differentiated classroom. We don't pretend to provide one. Our goal is to think aloud from the principles that govern our experiences, invite you to think along with us, and discover ways to expand your capacity as a teacher who works tirelessly to make room for each student.

For us, this is an "aspirational guide." We have no illusions that any teacher—even the best among us—reads a book and emerges with a radically different teaching style in tow. We do believe, however, that there are many teachers who aspire to grow as professionals every day. We believe there are teachers who will read and reread ideas in pursuit of understanding and insight. We believe there are teachers who, despite powerful forces to the contrary, will act with professional integrity in their classrooms and give reality to both deeply held and emerging beliefs to benefit their students. We believe those teachers exist because we have been taught by them and watched them teach. We've written this book for those aspirational teachers who mean to change themselves and their students—and do.

Carol Tomlinson

Part I

Leading a
Differentiated Classroom

The teacher's overriding moral purpose is to meet the needs of students, even when it conflicts with personal preferences.

—Lorna Earle, *Assessment as Learning*

A chorus of voices—representative of experts in virtually every aspect of education—continually asserts that current ideas about "how to do school" are inadequate both as a reflection of our current knowledge of teaching and learning and as a means to address the learning needs of an increasingly diverse student population. In terms of incorporating contemporary knowledge of how people learn into the classroom, experts make the analogy that we're settling for a Model-T Ford instead of drawing on 21st century automotive engineering.

More to the point, the old images of effective classrooms are anachronistic in terms of today's students and their needs. Not only do learners compose an increasingly diverse group, but they are also young people who live in a world of personalization—at least outside of school. They are accustomed to watching a particular television show when it's convenient rather than when it's broadcast. They no longer buy entire albums to "own" a particular song but rather download just the selections they like. They order computers specifically designed for their needs. They get news on demand and information they need when they need it. In school, however, we teach them as though their variance in readiness, individual interests, and particular approaches to learning were of no consequence. It is becoming increasingly difficult to pretend that batch processing of a vastly diverse student population supports them as learners or that we are preparing them for productive citizenship in a world with complexities, uncertainties, and challenges that demand the very best from each of them.

Consider the following excerpts from five current key educational documents in the United States. The first comes from the Interstate New Teacher Assessment and Support Consortium (INTASC) Standards and reflects professional consensus about what new teachers should know and be able to do, regardless of their specialty areas. The second comes from the National Board for Professional Teaching Standards—the body that provides the framework for National Board certification of top teachers in the United States. The third through fifth excerpts come from the National Association for the Education of Young Children, the National Middle School Association, and the National Association of Secondary School Principals. This collection represents the sweep of professional expectations for teachers—novice to expert and preschool through high school—and the message is clear and consistent: Student differences matter and effective teachers attend to those differences thoughtfully and proactively.

Some expectations for new teachers

The candidate:

- Designs instruction appropriate to students' stages of development, learning styles, strengths, and needs.
- Selects approaches that provide opportunities for different performance modes.
- Accesses appropriate services or resources to meet exceptional learning needs when needed.
- Adjusts instruction to accommodate the learning differences or needs of students (time and circumstance of work, tasks assigned, communication and response modes).

- Uses knowledge of different cultural contexts within the community (socio-economic, ethnic, cultural) and connects with the learner through types of interaction and assignments.
- Creates a learning community that respects individual differences.
- Assumes different roles in the instructional process (instructor, facilitator, coach, audience) to accommodate content, purpose, and learner needs. (INTASC, 1992)

Some criteria for recognition as a National Board Certified Teacher

- National Board Certified Teachers (NBCTs) are dedicated to making knowledge accessible to all students. They believe all students can learn.
- They treat students equitably. They recognize the individual differences that distinguish their students from one another and they take account of these differences in their practice.
- They respect the cultural and family differences students bring to their classroom.
- NBCTs know how to assess the progress of individual students as well as the class as a whole. (National Board for Professional Teaching Standards, 2010)

Some expectations for early childhood educators

The face of America is rapidly changing. In three states, European-Americans are no longer the majority group. U.S. babies born today will reach adulthood in a country in which no one ethnic group predominates. By the year 2005, children and adolescents of color will represent 40% of all U.S. school children. The largest proportion of individuals with disabilities is found in the preschool population. Thus, tomorrow's early childhood teachers must be prepared to serve and to value a far more diverse group of young children and families than at any time in the past. (National Association for the Education of Young Children, 2001)

- Development and learning proceed at varying rates from child to child, as well as at uneven rates across different areas of a child's individual functioning. Individual variation has at least two dimensions: the inevitable variability around the typical or normative course of development and the uniqueness of each child as an individual. Children's development follows individual patterns and timing; children also vary in temperament, personality, and aptitudes, as well as in what they learn in their family and within the social and cultural context or contexts that shape their experience.

• All children have their own strengths, needs, and interests. Given the enormous variation among children of the same chronological age, a child's age is only a crude index of developmental abilities and interests. For children who have special learning needs or abilities, additional efforts and resources may be necessary to optimize their development and learning. The same is true when children's prior experiences do not give them the knowledge and skills they need to thrive in a specific learning environment. Given this normal range of variation, decisions about curriculum, teaching, and interactions with children should be as individualized as possible. Rigid expectations of group norms do not reflect what is known about real differences in development and learning. At the same time, having high expectations for all children is essential, as is using the strategies and providing the resources necessary to help them meet these expectations.

• To be effective, teachers must get to know each child in the group well. They do this using a variety of methods—such as observation, clinical interview (an extended dialogue in which the adult seeks to discern the child's concepts or strategies), examination of children's work, individual child assessments, and talking with families. From the information and insights gathered, teachers make plans and adjustments to promote each child's individual development and learning as fully as possible. Developmental variation among children is the norm, and any one child's progress also will vary across domains and disciplines, contexts, and time.

• Children differ in many other respects, too—including in their strengths, interests, and preferences; personalities and approaches to learning; and knowledge, skills, and abilities based on prior experiences. Children may also have special learning needs; sometimes these have been diagnosed and sometimes they have not. Among the factors that teachers need to consider as they seek to optimize a child's school adjustment and learning are circumstances such as living in poverty or homelessness, having to move frequently, and other challenging situations. Responding to each child as an individual is fundamental to developmentally appropriate practice. (National Association for the Education of Young Children, 2009)

Some descriptors of quality middle school teachers

• Teaching and learning approaches should accommodate the diverse skills, abilities, and prior knowledge of young adolescents; cultivate multiple intelligences; draw upon students' individual learning styles; and utilize digital tools. When learning experiences capitalize on students' cultural, experiential, and personal backgrounds, new concepts are built on knowledge students already possess.

- Continuous, authentic, and appropriate assessment measures, including both formative and summative ones, provide evidence about every student's learning progress. Such information helps students, teachers, and family members select immediate learning goals and plan further education. (National Middle School Association, 2010)

Some guidelines for high school teachers

It is inconvenient that no two students are exactly alike and that no individual student stays exactly the same over her or his travel through the high school years. [However,] batch processing does not work, at least for most adolescents. Personalization is a necessity. . . . While our students differ in wonderful (and sometimes exasperating) ways, we serve them well by taking a "core mission" and playing it out in teaching and learning that reflects each student's strengths and weaknesses, learning styles, and special needs. The mission has to be lean and focused; the necessarily rich variety emerges from individual students' interests, abilities, and weaknesses, as these wax and wane over time. It requires that each student be known well. Student "anonymity" has been the most consistent criticism of America's high schools. It must end, whatever it takes. (National Association of Secondary School Principals, 2004)

- Many reports have been issued in the past few years that reveal deep problems with the achievement levels of U.S. high school students as compared to international students. There is also a significant achievement gap along race and income lines as well as low graduation and college attendance rates for low income and minorities. More often than not, these low rates can be traced back to the large numbers of students entering high schools reading below grade level. The vast majority of high schools, to a great degree, have a climate of anonymity where little focus is placed on identifying the personal learning needs of individual students and using such information to foster improved teaching and learning.

- To be fully committed to high school reform, we must systemically reculture and improve the high school. The historical structure and purpose of the U.S. high school is no longer adequate to serve the needs of all of the nation's youth and provide them with the skills necessary to compete in the global marketplace of the 21st century. Significant improvement is needed, but such improvement can only be attained through a substantial change in the structure and culture of the high school. We recommend this be accomplished through support for

  - Increased academic rigor that reflects the integration of curriculum, instruction, and assessment.

• Personalized instruction and learning that is based on the academic needs of individual students.

• Schoolwide initiatives to improve reading and writing literacy skills. (National Association of Secondary School Principals, 2005)

These voices—which represent the best thinking in our profession—tell us unequivocally that student differences do matter and that quality teaching makes room for these differences. Yet, despite the consistent and often urgent calls for teachers to attend to individual learners' needs, and in spite of daily evidence that one-size-fits-all instruction fails many, if not most, students, it is extraordinarily difficult for us to pull away from antiquated conceptions and embrace more contemporary and effective ways of thinking about teaching and learning. There are many reasons why the idea of teaching with the individual in mind is challenging (if not confounding), not the least of which are classroom images that are indelible in the minds of teachers, students, and parents alike.

These familiar images and impressions have become second nature to so many of us because they are continually reinforced throughout our young lives. We all think we know the right way "to do school." Even very young children who play school at home know the rules: The "teacher" is in charge and the "students" sit silently in straight rows and watch the teacher, who tells the students what to learn. Students learn what they're told and repeat it back to the teacher. The teacher teaches everyone alike (which is only fair), and students who can't follow the rules or get restless with the routine get booted "out of class."

While this description may sound like a caricature of an actual classroom, it represents a set of beliefs about teaching and learning that are deeply embedded in most people. Whether we are teachers, parents, or students, these beliefs are a common set of blueprints for thinking about the right way "to do school"; it is difficult to conceive of the classroom in any other way. Nevertheless, if we aspire to teach so that our students are prepared to assume leadership roles in a world that is quite different from the factory-based era that the current model of schooling was designed to serve, learner-focused change is not an option, but an imperative.

Classroom Teachers as Leaders for Change

Responsibility for supporting change toward student-focused instruction belongs to many kinds of educators. Superintendents, principals, curriculum coordinators, specialists, grade-level coordinators, department chairs, media directors, and counselors are some of the educational players who have pivotal roles to play in recrafting classrooms so that they more effectively teach the diverse learners that populate them. This job is vastly easier when everyone works as a team toward a shared goal, and it is unacceptable for anyone in the chain to abdicate his or her responsibility to make school work for each student who enters the door. Nonetheless, the role of the classroom teacher in bringing about such change is central. No one else is as vital. If every other educator fails to assume the responsibility of leadership for student-focused change, the classroom teacher still has the power to reenvision and reinvent teaching and learning.

It is the classroom teacher who has an unspoken contract with each learner to make productive use of time spent in the classroom. It is the classroom teacher who is in a unique position to see beyond multilayered distractions and disguises to know each learner as an individual human being. It is the classroom teacher who identifies or creates the links that exist between each individual learner and the critical content. It is the classroom teacher who taps into hidden motivations, builds bridges to span damaged trust, and reveals to each student how the learning process makes us fully human. Quite simply, the classroom teacher is an irreplaceable leader in moving differentiation from an abstract idea on paper or in a professional development session to a fundamental way of life in the classroom.

This book will highlight four different audiences for which teacher leadership is essential to make student-focused instruction a reality. First, teachers must do the daily work of motivating *themselves* to plan and implement instruction that keeps students in the foreground and of primary concern. Second, teachers must motivate, lead, and direct *students* to understand, contribute to, and participate in a classroom that is designed to take into account the needs of individuals and the group. Third, teachers need to lead *parents* to understand the goals of a student-focused or responsive classroom, how those goals will benefit their children, and how they can contribute to the success of their children and of the classroom. Finally, teachers can be important leaders for *other teachers* and for *school administrators* in understanding and contributing intelligently to academically responsive instruction.

Successful teachers are natural leaders. Along the way, we manage the details necessary to achieve goals that we have every reason to believe will benefit those who follow us. Genuine leadership indicates an ethical orientation—one that merits the trust of followers. To achieve such a level of leadership, we must

- Work from and aspire to an objective that is an improvement over the status quo.

• Articulate this vision so that those who are asked to follow have a compelling reason to do so.

• Move knowledgeably toward this vision while simultaneously attending to the voices and needs of those who will necessarily help enact it.

• Be patient with and supportive of followers, yet impatient with artificial barriers to progress.

• Maintain a pace that consistently ensures visible progress without pushing the system beyond its capacity to change.

• Monitor outcomes of the change and be willing to adapt, when necessary, to achieve desirable outcomes and eliminate undesirable outcomes.

Teacher Leadership for Differentiated Classrooms

The three chapters in Part I of this book are designed to help teachers be more confident and effective leaders for and in student-focused/responsive/differentiated classrooms. We do not presume that these chapters contain all there is to know about the topics they address. We are aware that each chapter provides, at best, an overview of a much more complex issue. We also know that individuals who invest their energies in any approach continue to transform and augment that approach. Our goal, then, is not to present the final word in regard to teacher leadership for differentiation but rather offer a framework for an intelligent beginning.

In our experience, teachers who are most effective with differentiation operate from strong (and growing) knowledge bases that are rooted in a philosophy of what classrooms could be like if they maximized the capacity of each learner. These teachers invite learners to help them construct such a classroom and to attend to its health as the academic year progresses. For these teachers, differentiation is not a set of strategies but rather a demographically necessary, ethically focused, pedagogically informed, and empirically tested way of thinking about the work they do.

Effective leaders are knowledgeable about and continue to nurture their knowledge of the area(s) in which they seek to lead. Chapter 1 reviews the elements of differentiated instruction for teachers who want to lead toward differentiation. Effective leaders work from a philosophy or belief system that informs the vision they commend to others. Chapter 2 articulates the philosophy that undergirds what we call "differentiation" so that teachers who seek to lead toward differentiation are grounded in their own views on teaching. Leaders engage followers in understanding and contributing to a shared vision. Chapter 3 provides suggestions for talking with students, parents, and other educators about differentiation so that teacher leaders can confidently invite them to participate in creating a place and processes that benefit the broadest possible array of learners. Chapters in the second half of the book focus on managing a differentiated classroom—a task made much easier and more reasoned when the teacher is first a leader for differentiation.

1

Understanding Differentiation in Order to Lead
Aiming for Fidelity to a Model

Few would argue that opportunity in life is strongly connected with educational opportunity. However, we have often misconstrued the notion of equal access to education to mean that all students should receive precisely the same pacing, resources, and instruction. The result is a one-size-fits-all education system. Differentiated instruction recognizes that students are not the same and that access to equal education necessarily means that, given a certain goal, each student should be provided resources, instruction, and support to help them meet that objective.

—John Stroup, University of Virginia doctoral student

"My district wanted all of its teachers to differentiate instruction," the young woman told me, "so they created a notebook of strategies for us. It's really nice. It's bound and everything. I guess it must have a dozen strategies in it."

"I'm glad you found it useful," I responded.

She paused as she searched for her next comment. "I did find it useful," she said. "I used every one of the ideas. And now I guess I'm just waiting for the next notebook."

She was puzzled. She had "done differentiation" cover to cover and had no idea where to go next. Because she had no basis for understanding how the ideas in the notebook had been generated, she was left feeling as if she had no basis for charting her own growth. She was experiencing what Ralph Waldo Emerson understood when he cautioned that if we only learn methods, we are tied to those methods, but if we learn principles, we can develop our own methods. My conversation with the young teacher reflected several common misunderstandings about differentiation:

1. **Misunderstanding:** Differentiation is a set of instructional strategies.

   Reality: Differentiation is a philosophy—a way of thinking about teaching and learning. It is, in fact, a set of principles.

2. **Misunderstanding:** It's adequate for a district or school leader (or professional developers) to tell, or even show, teachers how to differentiate instruction effectively.

   Reality: Learning to differentiate instruction well requires rethinking one's classroom practice and results from an ongoing process of trial, reflection, and adjustment in the classroom itself.

3. **Misunderstanding:** Differentiation is something a teacher does or doesn't do (as in, "I already do that," or "I tell our teachers that they already differentiate instruction.").

   Reality: Most teachers who remain in a classroom for longer than a day *do* pay attention to student variation and respond to it in some way—especially with students who can threaten order in the classroom. However, very few teachers proactively plan instruction to consistently address student differences in readiness, interest, and learning profile.

4. **Misunderstanding:** Differentiation is just about instruction.

   Reality: Although differentiation is an instructional approach, effective differentiated instruction is inseparable from a positive learning environment, high-quality curriculum, assessment to inform teacher decision making, and flexible classroom management. To the degree that any one of those elements is weak, the others are also diminished.

The purpose of this chapter is to provide a brief summary of what we call differentiated instruction; a full explanation of the elements of this approach is available in other resources (e.g., Tomlinson, 1999, 2001, 2004; Tomlinson, Brimijoin, & Narvaez, 2008; Tomlinson & McTighe, 2006). A clear understanding of the individual elements of differentiation, and how they relate to and shape the classroom system, paves the way for a more robust exploration of the philosophy of differentiation (which directs how teachers manage and lead an effectively differentiated classroom). The following two chapters should eliminate misunderstandings about differentiation—such as those noted above—and help prepare teachers to be effective leaders for differentiation in their classrooms and schools.

Key Elements of Differentiated Instruction

Differentiation can be accurately described as classroom practice with a balanced emphasis on individual students and course content. In other words, in an effectively differentiated classroom, it is understood that

- Students differ as learners in terms of background experience, culture, language, gender, interests, readiness to learn, modes of learning, speed of learning, support systems for learning, self-awareness as a learner, confidence as a learner, independence as a learner, and a host of other ways.

- Differences profoundly impact how students learn and the nature of scaffolding they will need at various points in the learning process.

- Teachers have a responsibility to ensure that all of their students master important content.

- Teachers have to make specific and continually evolving plans to connect each learner with key content.

- Teachers are required to understand the nature of each of their students, in addition to the nature of the content they teach.

- A flexible approach to teaching "makes room" for student variance.

- Teachers should continually ask, "What does *this* student need at *this* moment in order to be able to progress with *this* key content, and what do I need to do to make that happen?"

At the core of the classroom practice of differentiation is the modification of four curriculum-related elements—content, process, product, and affect—which are based on three categories of student need and variance—readiness, interest, and learning profile.

Content

The knowledge, understanding, and skills we want students to learn.

During differentiation, we emphasize the methods that students use to access key content (e.g., independent reading, partner reading, text on tape, text with images, listening comprehension, online research, communication with experts, group demonstrations, small group instruction) rather than change the content itself (Tomlinson & McTighe, 2006). There are instances, however, when some students need to go back to prerequisite content in order to move ahead, when advanced learners need to move ahead before their classmates are ready to do so, and when student Individualized Education Programs (IEPs) direct the teacher to change the content itself.

Process

How students come to understand or make sense of the content.

Real learning—of the sort that enables students to retain, apply, and transfer content—has to happen *in* students, not *to* them (National Research Council, 2000; Wiggins & McTighe, 1998). The word *process* is often used as a synonym for *activities*. However, activities can be misaligned with content goals and fail to require students to think through, grapple with, or use essential knowledge, understanding, and skills. Therefore, it is wise to substitute the term *sense-making activities* to emphasize that what we ask students to do in the name of learning or practice should help them "own" the content, see how it makes sense, and realize how it is useful in the world outside the classroom.

Product

How students demonstrate what they have come to know, understand, and are able to do after an extended period of learning.

A product is not something students generate in a single lesson or as a result of an activity or two. Rather, it is a rich culminating assessment that calls on students to apply and extend what they have learned over a period of time. Tests have these characteristics when they present students with complex problems to solve or issues to address in ways that require understanding of key ideas, transfer of knowledge, and application of skills. Effectively designed authentic assessments inevitably have these characteristics.

Affect

How students' emotions and feelings impact their learning.

Emotions and feelings originate in the brain based on past experiences and reactions to current experiences. They impact our motivation to learn, ability to work with others, and self-concept as a learner. In that way, affect is integral to, rather than apart from, curriculum. When a student has a positive affect regarding learning and himself or herself as a learner, it opens the door to academic growth. Conversely, a student's negative affect regarding learning or his or her own abilities as a learner shuts the door. Expert teachers don't just observe student behavior; they work to understand the affect that drives behavior so they can guide students in a positive direction.

Readiness

A student's current proximity to specified knowledge, understanding, and skills.

It is important to keep in mind that readiness is not a synonym for ability, and the two terms should not be used interchangeably. The term *ability* connotes what we sometimes believe to be a more or less fixed and inborn trait. *Readiness* suggests a temporary condition that should change regularly as a result of high-quality teaching. You'll see, as this chapter continues, that thinking in terms of "student readiness" rather than "student ability" is beneficial to both student and teacher. To grow academically, students must work consistently with tasks that are sharply focused on essential knowledge, understanding, or skills and that are a bit too difficult for their current level of readiness. In addition, students must have a support system in the form of peers and/or teachers who will help them surmount this difficulty and emerge from the task (or sequence of tasks) at a new and more advanced level of readiness (Sousa, 2001; Vygotsky, 1978, 1986; Wolfe, 2010).

Interest

That which engages the attention, curiosity, and involvement of a student.

Student interest is tied directly to student motivation to learn (Collins & Amabile, 1999; Csikszentmihalyi, 1990). When student interest is engaged, motivation to learn is heightened, and learning is enhanced. Personal interests are typically linked to a student's strengths, cultural context, personal experiences, questions, or sense of need.

Learning profile

A preference for taking in, exploring, or expressing content.

A student's learning profile is shaped by four elements and the interactions among them:

1. Learning style—A preferred contextual approach to learning. Learning styles include working alone or with a partner, in a quiet place or with music playing, in a bright room or a darkened environment, while sitting still or moving around (Dunn & Dunn, 1992, 1993; Gregorc, 1979).

2. Intelligence preference—A hard-wired or neurologically shaped preference for learning or thinking. For example, intelligence preferences include verbal-linguistic, logical-mathematical, kinesthetic, interpersonal, intra-personal, musical-rhythmic, spatial, analytical, practical, creative (Gardner, 1985; Sternberg, 1985).

3. Gender—Approaches to learning that may be shaped genetically or socially for males versus females. While not all males (or females) learn in the same ways, there are gender-based patterns of learning, and it may be advanta-geous to utilize teaching and learning options that reflect a range of gender-based preferences while we continue to enhance our understanding of ways in which gender and learning are interrelated (Gilligan, 1982; Gurian, 2001; Tannen, 1990).

4. Culture—Approaches to learning that may be strongly shaped by the context in which an individual lives and by the unique ways in which people in that context make sense of and live their lives. For example, how people communicate, relate to one another across generations, envision power structures, celebrate and mourn, and show respect are shaped by culture. As they do between genders, patterns of learn-ing vary somewhat across cultures, but it is not the case that all indi-viduals from a given culture approach learning in the same way. Thus, it is likely advantageous to student learning for a teacher to provide a range of teaching and learning approaches that, in turn, reflect a range of

culture-based learning preferences. In order to do this, it is essential that teachers study the diverse cultures of the students they teach so they can achieve a more multidimensional understanding of the relationship between culture and learning (Delpit, 1995; Heath, 1983; Lasley, Matczynski, & Rowley, 1997).

A teacher in an effectively differentiated classroom seeks to develop increasing insight into students' readiness levels, interests, and learning profiles. In order to develop instruction that maximizes each student's opportunity for academic growth, the teacher then modifies content, process, product, and affect. Figure 1.1 provides specific examples of how this can play out in the classroom for content, process, and product. By contrast, attending to students' affective needs generally

---

Figure 1.1
Examples of Differentiation Based on Student Need

	Readiness	Interest	Learning Profile
Content	• materials at varied readability levels • spelling assigned by proficiency • alternate presentation methods • targeted small group instruction • front-loading vocabulary • highlighted texts	• range of materials that apply key ideas and skills to a variety of real-world situations • teacher presentations designed to link to student interests	• varied teaching modes (e.g., verbal, visual, rhythmic, practical) • video or audio notes for students who learn better with repeated listening
Process	• tiered activities • mini-workshops • flexible use of time • learning contracts • varied homework assignments • RAFT options	• expert groups • interest centers • supplementary materials based on student interests • jigsaw • independent studies • interest-based application options • RAFT options	• choice of working conditions (e.g., alone or with a partner) • tasks designed around intelligence preferences • RAFT options • blogs and vlogs to share ideas
Product	• tiered products • personal goal-setting • varied resource options • check-in requirements based on student independence • providing samples of good student work at varied levels of complexity	• use of student interests in designing products • Design a Day options • use of contemporary technologies for student expression	• Complex Instruction • varied formats for expressing key content • varied working arrangements • varied modes of expressing learning

occurs when a teacher adapts the learning environment rather than the other three classroom elements.

Differentiation and the Classroom System

Differentiated instruction is a principle-guided method to approach teaching and learning, and it is implemented in the context of a classroom system that contains four interdependent elements: learning environment, curriculum, assessment, and instruction. In all classrooms, there is a learning environment that is shaped by a teacher's beliefs, experiences, and actions. There is a curriculum, shaped by a teacher's content knowledge, text materials, and local or federal mandates. There is some form of assessment, again shaped by both the teacher and forces external to the teacher. Finally, all classrooms benefit from instruction that individual teachers design (or follow established designs for) and implement. The way in which the teacher envisions and enacts each of these elements shapes each of the other elements. For example, an assessment that feels judgmental to students will negatively impact the learning environment. Likewise, a classroom in which curriculum is highly prescribed, with few or no options for a teacher to make professional decisions on behalf of students, limits that teacher's options for instruction.

The model of differentiation supported in this book adopts the position that each of these four elements must be shaped and cultivated to provide opportunities for every student to maximize his or her learning capacity. Only when each of the elements—separately and in conjunction with one another—supports maximum learning for each student is the classroom functioning as it should.

Learning environment

The physical and emotional context in which learning occurs.

The appearance, organization, and structure of a classroom can invite learning with appealing colors, effective displays of student work, spaces for both solitary and collaborative work, easy access to materials and supplies, furniture arrangements that focus attention on peer input rather than largely or solely on the teacher, and visible cues to support quality work. Conversely, a classroom's physical environment can diminish learning by being barren, drab, cramped, teacher-focused, distracting, or limiting (with seating arrangements that isolate students from one another). More significant than this physical climate, however, is the classroom's more intangible emotional climate. Students learn best when they feel safe, respected, involved, challenged, and supported. Thus, a learning environment that invites each student to be a full participant in the classroom—with full support for the journey—is a necessity for robust differentiated instruction.

Effective differentiation—in other words, effective attention to the learning needs of each student—requires a learning environment in which

- The teacher is attuned and responsive to the affective, cognitive, and physical needs of learners.
- Students feel safe, both physically and affectively.
- The teacher respects and supports the possibilities inherent in each student.
- Individual differences are accepted as natural and positive.
- Students learn to respect and support one another as learners.
- The teacher and students share in the decision-making process about daily routines and classroom operation.
- Hard work is an expectation.
- Physical arrangements are flexible and support student access to a variety of learning options.
- A range of resources are available and support student access to content.
- Flexible student grouping capitalizes on student strengths and allows effective attention to student weaknesses.

Curriculum

An organized plan to engage learners with important knowledge, understanding, and skills.

A list of standards is not a curriculum. A textbook is not a curriculum. These are ingredients—resources necessary for developing a curriculum. A high-quality curriculum begins with a teacher's sense of the authentic nature of the discipline that the curriculum will represent. It includes a clear delineation of the essential knowledge students should have and the skills they should possess as the result of a particular segment of learning (e.g., a year, a unit of study). It includes summative assessment mechanisms for determining student proficiency with designated outcomes that are tightly aligned with those assessments. It includes a carefully planned sequence of lessons or learning experiences that are designed to engage students with essential content and to ensure student success with the essential knowledge, understanding, and skills (Erickson, 2006; Tomlinson et al., 2009; Wiggins & McTighe, 2005).

The model of differentiation represented in this book advocates that all students (unless an IEP indicates otherwise) should

- Work with the essential knowledge, understanding, and skills in a lesson and unit of study.
- Be expected to think, and be supported as thinkers, as they engage with curriculum.
- Work with respectful tasks (i.e., tasks that are equally interesting and engaging, and those that promote understanding of, and the ability to apply, essential content).

Assessment

A data-gathering and analysis process that determines the degree to which students have achieved essential outcomes and informs decisions about and planning for instruction.

There are three kinds of assessment: (1) diagnostic assessment (preassessment), designed to determine a student's status relative to essential learning outcomes as a unit of study begins; (2) formative (ongoing) assessment, designed to follow a student's progress as he or she attains essential outcomes as a unit of study progresses; and (3) summative assessment, designed to measure student outcomes as a unit of study ends or at other key points in a unit or year of study.

High-quality assessments should guide students in understanding essential learning outcomes, their status relative to those outcomes, and ways in which they can work effectively to maximize their growth toward and beyond those outcomes (Earl, 2003). The model of differentiation on which this book is based emphasizes the use of

- Diagnostic assessments (preassessments) to determine individual students' entry points into a unit of study in terms of their readiness, interest, and learning profiles. This process is essential to planning for student variance.
- Formative assessments to measure students' readiness, interest, and learning profiles. This process is essential to planning for and supporting student variance.
- Summative assessments to offer varied modes of expression and scaffolding (based on students' needs in terms of language, time allocation, writing, etc.).

This process helps students express what they know, understand, and can do relative to essential outcomes.

Instruction

The process of teaching, educating, and engaging students with content.

Instruction is what many people think of when they think about teaching. It is the mechanism used to "deliver" the curriculum—or, more accurately, it connects content and learners. It positions the teacher as a metaphorical "bridge," helping students connect the knowledge and skills they already know (or are currently learning) to the essential outcomes they need in order to continue developing as learners and human beings. It helps develop an appropriate "game plan" to develop students' knowledge, self-awareness, and independence.

The model of differentiation on which this book is based advocates that instruction will

- Align with essential knowledge, understanding, and skills.
- Be designed with student differences in mind, including differences in learning, culture, language, and gender.
- Be flexible in terms of time, materials, support systems, student groupings, instructional modes, and teaching and learning strategies.
- Offer various routes to accomplishing essential learning outcomes.
- Help students develop self-efficacy and independence as learners.
- Help students develop proficiency in collaborative learning.
- Provide classroom routines that balance student needs for guidance and freedom.

Interdependence of Classroom Elements

It's likely that many of us began our teaching careers without a clear vocabulary to think about the key classroom elements described in this chapter. It's also likely that we weren't aware how each action we take ripples into all corners of the classroom. Over time, and as we became thoughtful and mindful professionals, we gradually developed a general awareness that our mood and energy levels set in motion "weather fronts" that permeate through the day and affect our students. Our weariness settles on students like fog; our joy becomes their excitement. A test that we have made to seem ominous can bring with it a storm cloud that threatens an otherwise hospitable atmosphere. Our capacity to peacefully disarm a crisis with one student makes the overall learning environment seem more secure for all students in it.

As we continue to develop as professionals, we become more cognizant of how the classroom elements interact. For example, we recognize that if a student feels like an outsider in the classroom, he or she is unlikely to commit to class discussions, group work, or even individual tasks, and this unfavorable learning environment negatively impacts curriculum and instruction for that student. Likewise, if assigned work is beyond the abilities of certain students, they will feel unsafe in the classroom and regard the learning environment as negative.

With time and experience, we are able to anticipate such situations and be proactive with specific and precise strategies to avoid them. For example, if we provide diagrams and images to ensure that students understand a difficult process before they read the relevant material in their texts, even students who typically resist such independent reading will likely feel that they have a better understanding of what they read. Careful instruction, then, improves the likelihood of a positive experience with curriculum. Figure 1.2 represents the Möbius-like interdependence among curriculum, assessment, and instruction—surrounded by aspects of the learning environment.

Figure 1.2
Interdependence of Key Classroom Elements

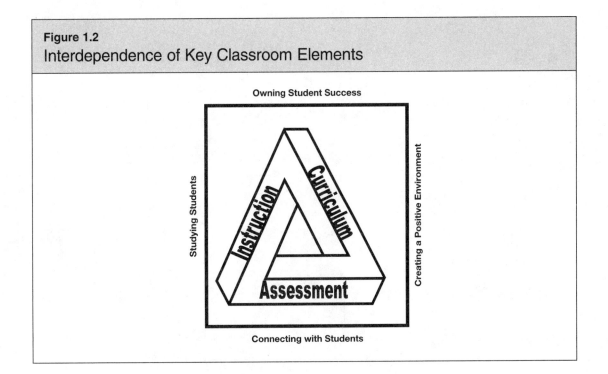

The contents of this chapter represent *what* teachers in successfully differentiated classrooms must create, monitor, and sculpt in order to support the best possible learning outcome for each student. These are the raw materials of teaching. The contents of Chapter 2 will examine *why* teachers in effectively differentiated classrooms think about their classrooms in the ways that they do, and it will focus on the philosophical underpinnings of differentiation. Comfort with both the *what* and *why* is important in a teacher's ability to lead for differentiation.

2

Teaching What You Believe
A Philosophy to Guide Teachers
Who Lead for Differentiation

When the school bell rings on day one and all our students are in their seats, we will hold the future of this nation and this world in our hands. Whatever we do will have lasting implications, not only on the lives of those students, but also on the lives of all those who they come in contact with. So then, the questions that we should ask ourselves should not be, "How can I make this work?" The question must be, "How can I afford not to make this work?"

—Wendy Kopp, *One Day, All Children*

Few, if any, teachers enter the profession with a well-developed philosophy of teaching. A meaningful philosophy of teaching develops silently, day by day, through crisis and triumph for those teachers who are willing to risk reflection about their work and their own role in that work. Experts who study change tell us that we can believe our way into new actions or act our way into new beliefs. Some feel it's more common for actions to shape our beliefs than the other way around (e.g., Fullan, 2007; Reeves, 2009). In other words, when a teacher tries something in a classroom and finds it beneficial to his or her students, that action shapes the teacher's beliefs about what works and how an effective classroom proceeds.

If teachers were required to enter their first classroom with the philosophical tenets of differentiation fully in tow, we would have no teachers. Our best hope for classrooms that work effectively for each student is to cultivate teachers who care deeply about teaching and the young people they teach; who believe teaching is a calling, not just a job; and who understand that they will become self-actualized professionals (to the degree that they are able) who pave the way for their students to also become self-actualized. It is certainly the case that teachers who lead effectively for differentiation operate from a clear sense that classrooms should model a world in which learning is rewarding and in which mutual respect, persistent effort, and shared responsibility make everyone stronger.

It is possible to make a strong case for differentiation based on the demographics of contemporary classrooms and the needs of an increasingly diverse student population to function in an increasingly complex world (Marx, 2000). It is also possible to make a strong case for differentiation based on research (e.g., Tomlinson et al., 2003). We believe, however, that the practice of differentiation is rooted in a student-centered philosophy or ethic of teaching.

The goal in briefly examining the philosophy behind differentiation in this chapter is not to suggest that educators wait until they have this—or any other—belief system solidly in place before they try to address student learning needs. Rather, our hope is that reflecting on these ideas will be beneficial to teachers who want to lead for differentiation, helping them examine their own beliefs and understand some of the thinking that undergirds a coherent, determined, and proactive approach to differentiating instruction. This reflection should also help teachers develop a rationale or vision that will help them talk with their students about a differentiated classroom and make instructional decisions to benefit their students.

There are numerous ways to order the ideas that follow. The method we've chosen seems as logical as any, yet we know that these ideas do not evolve in a logical or even "step-wise" fashion for many teachers. We are aware that many of these beliefs are interconnected—they are difficult to separate from one another. We also recognize that we include only a sampling of insights in each area and invite readers to add their thinking to ours.

We'll begin by taking a look at some core tenets of the philosophy of differentiation. Then, we'll examine how those beliefs or principles might shape a teacher's affective response to his or her students' affective needs. Finally, we'll examine some concrete examples of how those principles might guide teachers' aspirations to establish, lead, and ultimately manage a differentiated classroom.

Beliefs That Point to Differentiated Instruction

Lorna Earl reflects, "Differentiation is making sure that the right students get the right learning tasks at the right time. Once you have a sense of what each student holds as 'given' or 'known' and what he or she needs in order to learn, differentiation is no longer an option. It is an obvious response" (2003, pp. 86–87).

This is an immensely practical way to look at differentiation, but it also models a useful cause-and-effect approach to thinking about the philosophical roots of differentiation. To take some liberties with her words, Earl is in essence saying that if we care about whether learning is working for each of our students, we must continue to monitor their growth in terms of what we deem to be critical learning goals. Inevitably, we'll find that students are in different places with their mastery of those goals. Then, as she suggests, because we want to make sure each student succeeds, we have no choice but to differentiate instruction. There's simply no alternative.

The belief that sets Earl's sequence of thoughts in motion is an affirmation in the profound worth of every learner—not a vague, generalized, mission-statement sort of belief. A belief in the worth of the individual propels a teacher to look "eyeball to eyeball" at the humanity of each student and dictate classroom practice as a result. The statement asks, "If you believe X, what choice do you have but Y?" Following is a set of beliefs leading to classroom practice that doggedly attend to the needs of individual learners because *there simply is no other choice.*

Belief 1: Every student is worthy of dignity and respect

At the center of democracy, and the world's major religions, resides a conviction that we should hold human life in esteem and regard it with a sense of awe. From this comes the admonition that each life is unique, irreplaceable, and innately valuable. In most societies, the mature individual is cast as one who can move beyond egocentrism to recognize and address the needs of others and can seek justice not just for oneself but for others. Words affirming human dignity surround us and are prevalent in government documents, houses of worship, judicial rulings, political conversations, and ethical debates. The danger, of course, is that although we "accept" the idea of human dignity almost automatically in much of the free world, we enact this idea with much greater difficulty.

The teacher who both accepts and enacts the principle of human dignity does not look at a class roster and simply see a list of names. That teacher considers teaching to be a stewardship of young lives—a shaping of them. He or she aspires to act and interact in ways that consistently respect and dignify the worth of each student. Such teachers accept the premise that teaching is essentially about building lives (Tompkins, 1996).

Much of the impetus for differentiated instruction is predicated on the belief that every young life is of ultimate value and should be treated accordingly by adults who have responsibility for shaping those lives. Decisions about classroom rules, curriculum, instruction, student groupings, discipline, grading, and virtually every other aspect of teaching are shaped by the centrality or marginality of this belief in a teacher's thinking. Attempting to enact this belief into classroom practice certainly does not simplify the teacher's role, but it likely does enrich it.

A belief in the worth and dignity of each student leads teachers to ask questions such as

- How can I gain an understanding of the particular talents, strengths, and needs of this student?
- In what ways can I show this student that I respect and value him/her?
- How do I help this student recognize and extend his/her strengths?
- How can I ensure my own cultural competence in order to be the most effective teacher possible for each learner?
- In what ways can I help students see and value the contributions and potential of every other student in the class?
- How can I guide development of a sense of classroom community characterized by respect?

Belief 2: Diversity is both inevitable and positive

A teacher created a poster that hung prominently in the front of her classroom. It read, "Our similarities make us human. Our differences make us individuals." Her conversations and actions with students persistently reaffirmed the words on the wall. She reminded her students that everyone needs kindness and friends. Everyone makes mistakes. Everyone has good days and bad. These are human things. However, Josh's sense of humor is uniquely his. Javier's Latino background means that he knows things others in the class might not, and the class can therefore learn from him. Andrea's perspectives as the oldest child in a large family help her see things in ways that her classmates might not think of.

Through this, the teacher helps her students learn a critical reality: We are a great deal alike as human beings and, in those ways, we share a common bond, yet human beings differ as well. Sometimes those differences separate us, but they don't need to. They should enrich us—and they do—when we are open to them.

A belief in diversity as both normal and positive leads teachers to ask questions such as

- How do I contribute to my students' awareness of their core similarities and their individuality?
- How do I seek diverse perspectives on issues and topics in our class?
- How do I help students learn to seek and value multiple perspectives on issues and topics?
- How well do I understand my own culture and how it shapes my perspectives and practices as a person and as a teacher?
- How do I ensure that all students' backgrounds, cultures, languages, patterns of communication, preferred ways of learning, and traditions are represented in our classroom's operation, curriculum, and materials?
- How do I ensure that each student has equity of access to the highest quality learning opportunities?
- How do I create group work that draws on the particular strengths of the group's members?
- How do I ensure that every student has a significant intellectual contribution to make to the work of the class?

Belief 3: The classroom should mirror the kind of society in which we want our students to live and lead

Certainly, we want young people to live in, value, and defend a society that accords respect and dignity to each of its members. We also live in a time when the world is rapidly becoming everyone's backyard. There is a new resident population in many parts of the United States that is an amalgam of languages, cultures, economic backgrounds, and possibilities. We therefore need classrooms in which students not only accept, but expect and value, diversity. Thus, the first two beliefs that lead to differentiation are tied to this third belief.

Vivian Paley (1993) saw her kindergartners beginning the practice of excluding peers from games and classroom groups. Understanding the long-term liabilities for both the rejected and the rejecter, she posted a new classroom rule: "You can't say you can't play." Over time, she helped her young students debate the fairness of exclusion. Though conducted in the language of 5-year-olds, the conversations initially sounded remarkably like adult rationales for sorting and separating people. In time, her students came to accept the rule, live by it, appreciate it, and defend it. Even at a young age, they found that it was not possible to simultaneously value and exclude a person or a group. They ultimately understood that if "different" meant you had to be somewhere else, then "different" wasn't a good thing. They came to see differences as just part of who they were rather than as reasons to suspect or reject one another.

Likewise, it is difficult to make a compelling argument that a school or teacher has deep regard for the value of each individual and accepts diversity as both normal and desirable while designating some students as "able" and others as "less able" for the purpose of dividing them academically. Our long-standing practices of academic segregation are complex and still advocated by many.

With regard to students with learning challenges, Richard Villa and Jacqueline Thousand remind us, "Inclusive education is about . . . making a commitment to provide each student in the community, each citizen in a democracy, with the inalienable right to belong. . . . Inclusion is the opposite of segregation and isolation. . . . Segregated education creates a permanent underclass of students and conveys to those students that they do not measure up, fit in, or belong" (2005, p. 5). The same could be said of students from low-income backgrounds, students whose first language is not English, students who live in foster care, and many other categories of learners who often find themselves excluded from "regular" classrooms, enriched reading groups, field trips, and other opportunities that indicate student status. To value is to include, not exclude. To honor diversity is to invite it, not shunt it away.

The belief that classrooms should mirror the world in which we hope our students can live and lead causes teachers to ask questions such as

- How do I come to understand my students' diverse backgrounds and needs so that I can draw on them and build on them effectively?

• How do my students and I create an inclusive learning environment in which they learn well together, not just occupy the same space?

• How do I help students create a classroom in which they understand that we all have different entry points into learning, yet share a common need to learn?

• How do students come to encourage and support one another's growth?

• How do students learn to celebrate one another's growth?

Belief 4: Most students can learn most things that are essential to a given area of study

Teacher beliefs about students' capacity to succeed are often buried beneath consciousness. Those beliefs are nonetheless powerful determinants in shaping both teaching and student attitudes about learning.

Carol Dweck, whose research on motivation spans several decades (e.g., 2000, 2006), tells us that we develop early in life a "mind-set" about what it means to be smart and how we become successful. Her work suggests two options, a fixed mind-set or a growth (fluid) mind-set. People who develop a fixed mind-set conclude that success comes from inborn ability—that is, a person is born smart or they aren't. People who develop a growth mind-set reach a different conclusion. They believe that success isn't determined by innate ability, but rather by persistent and informed effort—that is, people work their way to success.

Students with a fixed mind-set feel a sense of inevitability when they encounter difficulty in school. For example, students who struggle with school on a regular basis simply conclude that they can't succeed because they are not smart. Likewise, students who are highly able might balk at challenges because they believe smart people shouldn't have to work hard, and if they can't handle the challenge with minimal effort, then it's an indication that they aren't smart. In either case, students with fixed mind-sets have minimal motivation to work hard.

Students with a growth mind-set believe that if a skill or task is difficult, they can nonetheless achieve mastery because their continuing effort will win the day. Their motivation to work hard is high because they believe the payoff will be worth their investment.

Teachers with a fixed mind-set certainly "teach" all their students, but they do so with a sense that "some kids will get it, and some won't." In a way, these teachers teach without the expectation that every student will learn. They draw conclusions, often unconsciously and often early in a course or grade, about which students are smart and which are not. They then proceed to teach accordingly, remediating some students and enriching or accelerating others.

Teachers with a growth mind-set work from the premise that virtually any student can learn anything if the student is willing to work hard and if he or she has support in that effort. Such teachers aren't interested in labels or past performance; they simply set out to establish an ethic of hard work and teach students the skills they need to work effectively. Success with essential learning goals for each student is the only acceptable outcome for these teachers.

Not surprisingly, there is an interaction between the mind-sets held by both students and teachers. Figure 2.1 illustrates some of the possible interactions and implications.

It is important to note that Dweck finds people can and do change their mind-sets. Teachers with growth mind-sets regularly help students understand that they have control over their success, thus enabling students with fixed mind-sets begin to operate from a sense of personal agency.

The contribution of a growth mind-set to student motivation and achievement is considerable (e.g., Aronson, Fried, & Good, 2002; Good, Aronson, & Inzlicht, 2003). Students who come to believe that their hard work will positively impact their success earn higher achievement test scores and grades, engage in academics at a higher level, and enjoy the academic process more than students who retain a fixed mind-set perspective.

It is unlikely that a fixed mind-set teacher exerts enough effort to ensure the success of a student whom that teacher (consciously or unconsciously) believes

Figure 2.1
Possible Interactions Between Teacher and Student Mind-Set

		Fixed Mind-Set	Growth Mind-Set
STUDENT	**Growth Mind-Set**	Teacher may underestimate student capacity and willingness to work hard and "teach down" because of the student's language, culture, economic status, race, label, etc.	Both teacher and student study student growth, set goals for progress, and look for ways to continue development. Students at all readiness levels have maximum opportunity for challenge, growth, and success.
	Fixed Mind-Set	Both teacher and student accept the student's difficulties as given, and neither exerts the effort needed for high levels of student achievement. Both also accept high grades on grade-level work as adequate for advanced learners.	Teacher encourages and insists on student effort and growth. Over time, the student's mind-set can change to a growth orientation with evidence that effort leads to success. Students at all readiness levels have maximum opportunity for challenge, growth, and success.
		Fixed Mind-Set	**Growth Mind-Set**
		TEACHER	

Reprinted with permission from Solution Tree.

is incapable of success. Differentiation is a growth mind-set endeavor—it asks teachers to find an academic entry point relative to essential learning outcomes, to make instructional plans designed to move students to mastery of those outcomes, and to adopt a "whatever it takes" approach in doing so. It also calls on teachers to work with students to show them the direct link between effort and success, thus enlisting each student's energy in his or her own success.

Dweck counsels that we serve our students best not by telling them they are smart, but by being candid about where their skills are at a given time and where they need to be in order to achieve their life and school dreams. We also need to give students our assistance in developing the attitudes, work habits, and strategies necessary to accomplish their goals. She continues, "The confidence students need is not the confidence that they have a certain level of smartness, or that they have more of it than other students. The confidence they need is the confidence that they, or *anybody* for that matter, can learn if they apply their effort and strategies" (2000, pp. 57–58).

A belief in the capacity of virtually all students to learn essential content causes teachers to ask questions such as

- How do I understand the mind-set of each of my students in order to ensure that they understand their capacity to impact their own success?

- How do I help each student develop and extend the attitudes, habits of mind, and strategies needed to contribute to his or her success as a learner?

- How do I understand and address each student's learning development and needs relative to designated learning outcomes for my grade/subject(s)?

- How do I ensure that there are materials and support needed for each student's progress?

- How do I ensure that classroom working arrangements build on students' cultural preferences for learning?

- In what ways can I make clear to my students that I value their effort rather than their innate ability—that I am much more interested in their growth than about their starting points?

- How do I ensure that competition against oneself, rather than against one another, is the goal of this class?

- How do I ensure that student growth is a key and visible component in reporting grades?

Belief 5: Each student should have equity of access to excellent learning opportunities

A belief in the worth of each student should lead us to conclude that virtually every young person should have access to the best learning opportunities a school has to offer. To suggest that some students require less is to retrench on a deeply important ideal. As John Dewey remarks,

> What the best and wisest parent wants for his own child, that must the community want for all of its children. Any other ideal for our schools is narrow and unlovely; acted upon, it destroys our democracy. . . . Only by being true to the full growth of all the individuals who make it up, can society by any chance be true to itself. (Schlechty, 1997, p. 77)

A belief in the capacity of all students to learn the essential knowledge and skills in a topic or unit of study suggests that schools offer their very best to everyone. This belief also implies two additional assumptions. First, learning opportunities should focus on what is essential to learn—that is, on how the subject makes sense and what makes it authentic, useful, relevant, and meaningful. Second, the curriculum and instruction to which all learners are exposed should provide consistent opportunities to understand the content so students can retain, apply, and transfer what they learn (Tomlinson & McTighe, 2006). In other words, if our schools and teachers operated from a growth mind-set perspective, we would have little reason to assume that only a few students could learn conceptually, think critically, debate ideas, and address real-world issues. Rather than develop curriculum that mirrors a belief that only a relatively small proportion of students can do complex work, we would plan "high-end" curriculum for most students and then differentiate instruction to make certain each student is supported in achieving and, if possible, exceeding those complex goals.

There is ample evidence that the practice of providing high-quality curriculum and instruction for some—but not all—students results in an escalating disadvantage for students who are already at a disadvantage in terms of their opportunity to achieve (e.g., Carbonaro & Gamoran, 2002; Gamoran, Nystrand, Berends, & LePore, 1995). In addition, indications are increasingly clear that establishing expectations for a majority of students to become creators (rather than simply consumers) of knowledge is imperative if we expect all of our young people to thrive in and contribute to the world they will enter as they leave school (Marx, 2000). "In today's Information Age . . . educators must operate from the premise that it is the purpose of schools to bring all students to their full potential and to a level of education that was once reserved for the very few" (DuFour & Eaker, 1998, p. 62).

A belief in equity of access to excellent learning opportunities leads teachers to ask questions such as

- To what degree does the curriculum seem relevant to and engage each student in my class?
- Is the curriculum designed to ensure student understanding of content?
- Am I confident that I am "teaching up" to all of my students, rather than "watering down" for some of them?
- Are all of the tasks I offer respectful—that is, are they equally appealing and focused on essential understandings, do they require students to think critically and/or creatively, and do they ask all students to work with content in authentic ways?
- In what ways can I make certain that my most advanced students are being consistently challenged?
- In what ways can I support each student in achieving and, if possible, surpassing established goals?
- Is each student an active participant in discussions designed to help them make meaning of ideas?
- How do I schedule our time so students can focus on their own academic needs and still come together around important ideas?

Belief 6: A central goal of teaching is to maximize the capacity of each learner

Ensuring that each student experiences the best curriculum and instruction a school can offer, as well as the support necessary to succeed in such settings, would move schools much closer to this belief. In practice, however, we generally fall short of embracing it for at least two reasons. First, we tend to accept a single performance level as adequate or even desirable for a grade level. While it is clearly important to have specified learning targets for teachers and students, when we assume that all students reach their maximum respective potential if they achieve the same goals under the same circumstances on the same day, we operate in direct contradiction to all that we know about human development. While, for some students, success is inevitably out of reach on the date designated to judge their competence, other students are invariably determined to be successful without regard for the fact that they may have passed that performance level earlier in the year.

Students learn incrementally from their various starting points. It is simply how the process works. We cannot require students to make an impossible leap over a chasm in knowledge; nor should we ask them to move backwards in order to stay with the class. Theodore Sizer explains it this way:

> One cannot succeed at something totally beyond one's experience, beyond one's grasp. One is interested in that at which one succeeds. Thus, a clever teacher sets a student's work, and the expectations for it, at a level where some modicum of legitimate success is possible. However, because "experience has shown that it is worth the effort to provide the growing child with problems that tempt him into next stages of development," an effective teacher keeps the subject of study at an arm's length from the student, but no further. The joy of success comes especially sweet when that which was mastered had earlier seemed unachievable. (Sizer, 1985, p. 167)

Further, when we set a single benchmark for all students, it is inevitably a "middling" one. In doing so, we teach students that there is a finish line and that "good enough" is good enough. Former U.S. Secretary of Education John Gardner (1961) reminded us that we are in peril if the goal we set for ourselves is one of amicable mediocrity. All we can ask of a student is that he or she invests maximum effort in learning—and we should not settle for less from our students or from ourselves.

A second reason that our classrooms aren't geared to maximize the capacity of each learner is that we tend to see and think of our students as a group (Brighton, Hertberg, Moon, Tomlinson, & Callahan, 2005). We say, "*The students* always love it when we do this lab," or "*The students* don't understand inverting fractions," or "*The students* were restless today." No doubt a number of students *do* like the lab, *don't* understand how and when to invert fractions, and *were* restless today; but there's also little doubt that some students found the lab pointless or confusing, could teach a cogent lesson on inverting fractions, and were perfectly calm and ready to learn today. It's virtually impossible to attend to student differences when we think of "the students" as a single entity. Such thinking also reinforces the sense that a single learning indicator or set of indicators is appropriate for "the students" at a given time.

Differentiation asks teachers to look beyond "groupthink" and to study the evolving profiles of students as individuals. The degree to which a teacher melds respect for the individual and belief in the capacity of the individual to succeed with the intent to know each student as an individual determines the likelihood that the goal of maximizing the capacity of each learner is operationalized. Such a triumvirate of beliefs also results in many more students exceeding the unitary standard(s) we now establish.

A belief in the importance of maximizing the capacity of each learner leads teachers to ask questions such as

- What is this student's next step in learning essential content today?
- How can I help each student understand and contribute to his or her next step in learning?
- What task will push this student a bit beyond his or her comfort zone today?
- What models and indicators can I use to help this student understand what high-quality work looks like at his or her stage of growth?
- How can I tap into this student's motivation to strive for quality?
- What forms of support does this student need from me and from his or her peers to persist in the face of difficulty?
- How do we support one another in working for quality?
- How do we chart growth and quality over time?
- How do we recognize and celebrate excellence in ourselves individually and as a community of learners?

A Philosophical Compass for the Journey Ahead

Good teaching—the really good stuff—is hard work. Being a good teacher requires many of the same demands as being a good parent, a good doctor, or a good lawyer. Humans are largely sustained in our work by a belief that what we do makes a profound difference in the lives of other people. Differentiation is an individual-focused approach to teaching. It is the manifestation of a conviction that *every* student is both unique and of prime importance as a learner and as a human being. It is an affirmation that human differences are normal and desirable, and that excellent teachers plan, teach, and reflect with those differences in mind.

We will not successfully restructure schools to be effective until we stop seeing diversity in students as a problem. Our challenge is not one of getting "special" students to better adjust to the usual schoolwork, the usual teacher pace, or the usual tests. The challenge of schooling remains what it has been since the modern era began two centuries ago: ensuring that all students receive their entitlement. They have the *right* to thought-provoking and enabling schoolwork so that they might use their minds well and discover the joy therein to be willing to push themselves farther. They have the *right* to instruction that obligates the teacher, like the doctor, to change tactics when progress fails to occur. They have the *right* to assessment that provides students and teachers with insight into real-world standards. . . . Until such a time, we will have no insight into human potential. Until the challenge is met, schools will continue to reward the lucky or the already-equipped and weed out the poor performers. (Wiggins, 1992, pp. xv–xvi)

Enter the Students

A philosophy in the abstract is worthwhile since it grounds our thinking and reminds us that a life well lived or a career well spent is likely to be more reasoned and purposeful than random. The test of that philosophy comes in the arena of daily life rather than in the seclusion of individual minds. In the case of teaching, a defensible philosophy supports the capacity of teachers to address the needs of the young people they teach.

Abraham Maslow found that individuals develop along a continuum of needs, with the more basic human needs demanding attention before higher-level needs can be satisfied (1943). First in line, he tells us, are physiological needs for things such as food, clothing, shelter, and sleep. The primacy of these needs is so great that when there is a deficiency in one or more of them, the body focuses almost exclusively on attending to that need. In a school setting, students who enter the classroom hungry, cold, sleepy, or worried about where they will find shelter at night have no energy to learn a new language or complete a worksheet—until a teacher or another adult can attend to their needs.

Once physiological needs are met, the need for safety and security takes center stage. For these needs to be satisfied, students require a sense that they are physically safe, but also safe from teasing, bullying, and hopelessness in terms of the tasks and challenges ahead. A school and classroom that provide safety and demand respect can help pave the way to effective learning, but when the end of the day nears and the student again faces potential threats, anticipation of the dangers ahead will push learning aside. Only when safety and security seem assured can individuals systematically seek acknowledgment and belonging. Most students want to be part of a community. A feeling of collegiality or "teamwork" in the classroom satisfies this need to be a part of (rather than apart from) the group. The absence of such a sense of belonging leads to loneliness, isolation, and low self-esteem. In school, it essentially derails the learning process.

When an individual's physiological needs are adequately addressed, attention can then be spent on esteem needs such as academic learning. When this is the case, students demonstrate a desire to engage themselves in ways that bring recognition and value. They want to contribute and be valued as contributors to the group and its work. Through achievement, they develop a sense of self-efficacy.

The final two levels of Maslow's hierarchy of needs are self-actualization, in which an individual strives to become all that he or she can be, and self-transcendence, in which individuals learn to live at a higher level of insight and on a plane that takes them beyond themselves. It is highly unusual for young people to achieve these two stages.

It is interesting, then, to realize that academic learning requires students to work at the highest level of need satisfaction within their grasp. It certainly reminds us, once again, that a teacher's job is not simply to enter a room and impart knowledge, but rather to attend to each learner as a whole human being in order to expose him or her to learning.

Taking into account the progress of Maslow's hierarchy, it is likely that most learners come to school not to seek mastery of math or literature, but rather to address more basic needs first, such as affirmation and contribution. Once those needs have been met, they shift their attention to things such as purpose, challenge, and power (Tomlinson, 2004). A teacher who honors the individual seeks to understand each student's particular progression of needs and to address those needs in a way that leads to both personal and academic growth.

The Teacher Responds

Students *will* come to school with the sorts of needs—both cognitive and affective—outlined by Maslow. Teachers *will* respond to those needs—by addressing them or ignoring them, understanding the similarities and differences in how students experience them or generalizing across students. At least two elements determine a teacher's response to students' needs and its quality in terms of student benefits. One determinant is the philosophy (or lack thereof) that shapes the teacher's actions. The second determinant is the teacher's level of competency in setting and following a specific course of action. We often think of these two elements as "will" and "skill." Ultimately, a philosophy of teaching is based on a will to teach each learner.

We hope this chapter will contribute to the development of beliefs about the nature and purpose of teaching. We also hope that the following chapters will contribute to teachers' skills in managing and leading a classroom that is attentive to learners' particular needs and to the group's common needs. A philosophy of teaching based on beliefs such as the ones outlined earlier in this chapter leads teachers to respond to student needs for affirmation, purpose, challenge, and power with invitation, investment, persistence, opportunity, and reflection (Tomlinson, 2004). In a variety of ways and over time, teachers need to consistently convey the following messages to their students, both individually and as a whole class.

Invitation—I am pleased that you are here, eager to know you better, and aware that you bring important experiences and characteristics to class with you. I want to do whatever I can to make this a valuable place of learning for you.

Investment—Because you are important in this class and in the world, I am going to work hard to help you grow as much and as fast as you can. Because your effort has much to do with your success, I am going to ask you to work hard as well.

Persistence—You won't always get things right the first time you try them. Neither will I. When class is not going well for you, I am going to work for you and with you to find approaches that will ensure your success. I will never give up on you.

Opportunity—You are young and just learning about the possibilities that exist in the world. I want to provide opportunities for you to see yourself at work in varied settings, in varied roles, and with varied content. This is a time for you to prepare for the future and get excited by the possibilities that exist for you.

Reflection—I will listen to you, learn from you, observe you at work in our class, study your progress, and ask for your guidance. I will think about my work and how it's working for you as often as I possibly can. I expect that of myself so that I can become a more aware and effective teacher. I will ask the same of you so you can become a more aware and effective learner.

In addition to this sort of affective response to a student's needs, a teacher whose work is rooted in the worth of the individual understands that much of what he or she communicates to students will be in the form of curriculum and instruction. Therefore, the teacher ensures that every student's work is engaging, important, focused, challenging, and scaffolded (Tomlinson, 2004). These attributes of day-to-day work clearly communicate to students the teacher's belief in their individual worth and potential.

In a book that is both disturbing and hopeful, Kirsten Olson presents her body of research, which includes interviews with many adults from diverse backgrounds, virtually all of whom felt profoundly "wounded by school" (2009). She didn't set out to do research in this area. Rather, the work evolved as she discovered that many adults with whom she spoke (about other topics) discussed negative impacts that school had on them. She goes on to clarify that her definition of "wounded by school" does not include the inevitable moments of discomfort that occur when substantial numbers of young people share a classroom or the kinds of natural "bumps and bruises" that help us grow. Instead, she's talking about the hurt that diminishes individuals in their own eyes, that doesn't go away even in adulthood, and that cannot be dismissed even if the victim achieves success in the eyes of the world. Common results of such wounding that emerged from the interviews include

- A loss of pleasure in learning.
- A belief that we are not smart or competent in learning.
- A belief that our abilities are fixed and can't be improved with effort, coaching, or self-understanding.
- A belief that we are "just average" in a way that feels diminishing.
- Anger toward teachers and others in authority because we feel that we are not seen or acknowledged.
- A tendency to categorize people as "smart" or "dumb."
- A generalized feeling of shame that came from school and produces generalized anxiety.
- A sense that school diminished us cognitively.
- A low appetite for intellectual risk-taking; in other words, a desire to get the right answer and just finish the job.

Olson finds that there are some teachers who heal wounds, and as a group, they exhibit predictable behaviors. These teachers

- Welcome and honor difference in race, social class, gender, and sexual orientation.
- Accept many types of students and consciously value diversity of background and experience in the classroom.

- Place the student at the center of instruction.
- Honor what students already know and feel.
- Honor varied ways in which students most comfortably learn.
- Emphasize multiple avenues of content presentation, reflection, and assessment.
- Make communities of caring central to learning.
- Acknowledge the ambiguity inherent in teaching.
- Employ experimentation in instructional design and learn from mistakes.

It is not a great leap to suggest that a philosophy of differentiation exists to avoid wounding learners (as much as those wounds are within our power to avoid). Philosophically, differentiation is an approach that commends planning for human wholeness as a primary goal—and that provides for healing when necessary. Accepting this premise provides teachers with considerable guidance when they plan for instruction, reflect on instruction, and talk with others about the work they do. Chapter 3 will explore ways in which teachers invite students to share in the development of a philosophy of differentiation. It also examines how teachers assume the role as leader of parents, colleagues, and administrators in understanding and supporting differentiation.

3

The Invitation to Be Part of a Vision
Talking with Students, Parents, and Other Educators About Differentiation

Treating students as people comes very close to "living" the academic, personal, and social educational goals that are stated in most official policy documents. But more than that, involving students in constructing their own meaning and learning is fundamentally pedagogically essential—they learn more and are motivated to go even further.

—Michael Fullan, *The New Meaning of Educational Change, 3rd Edition*

A frequent comment from teachers who are early in their consideration of differentiation is "My students would be angry if they saw that someone else had a different book or a different activity than they did in a lesson." Interestingly, that is an issue almost never raised by teachers who are practitioners of differentiation. So why the difference?

Chances are good that the first teacher is operating from the common belief system about teaching and learning—and that his or her students are as well.

Among the tenets of that belief system is a common curriculum for everyone and, thus, a "right" or "standard" lesson that all students in the class must complete to ensure orderly coverage of the content. In that paradigm, a good teacher makes sure everyone does the same thing in a given lesson and uses a standard set of materials, standard pacing, and a standard support system. Not only is that the correct way "to do school," but it's also the "fair" way. Therefore, a teacher who does something different for one or a few students is at risk of being seen as unfair.

The second teacher is operating from a different belief system. This teacher believes that there is a common set of critical content that every student should learn and that his or her job as a teacher is to ensure that each student has the best possible opportunity to master and, if possible, move beyond that content. In this paradigm, it is understood that students enter each segment of learning at varied starting points, bring different experiences to which they can connect new learning, work at different speeds, process information in a variety of ways, and require different support systems in order to master the essential content. Thus, while this teacher is committed to ensuring that each student succeeds with designated learning outcomes, he or she also recognizes the need to provide a range of ways for students to access information, a variety of options for processing or making sense of the information, an array of support systems, and multiple outlets for students to demonstrate what they learn. In this teacher's way of thinking, treating all students exactly alike is counterproductive. It's necessary to meet students where they are in terms of readiness, interest, and learning profile in order to maximize their academic growth.

The first teacher envisions using a differentiated instructional strategy in an environment that values sameness—one where treating everyone alike is the gold standard—but it feels as though she'd be changing the rules of a game without telling the players, and she is pretty sure some level of anarchy would result. The second teacher is aware that most students come to her class with a standard set of rules firmly ingrained in their thinking (unless a prior teacher differentiated instruction or there is schoolwide attention to differentiation). This teacher, however, has no intention of trying to "sneak" differentiation into daily routines. She doesn't aspire to do differentiation *to* her students, but rather to do it *with* them. Therefore, from the first day of school, she sees her students as partners in her—and their own—success. From the first day of school, she works consistently to build a shared classroom vision and to construct with her students processes and procedures that support success of that vision. In other words, she will serve as a leader in establishing an effectively differentiated classroom.

This chapter will discuss specific goals for teachers who want to lead students and develop classrooms designed to support student success with critical content, specific ways in which teachers might engage their students in understanding and contributing to a differentiated classroom, and various conversations that enable teachers and students to develop a common sense of direction in the classroom. It will also briefly discuss the teacher as a leader in helping both parents and other educators understand and contribute to differentiation.

A Framework for Coming Together

At the beginning of the year, a teacher who wants to lead students to understand and contribute to a differentiated classroom will invest some start-up time to the process. There may be a few class periods or time slots that focus largely on conversations and activities related to differentiation, and there will be a number of others in which more abbreviated conversations or decision-making sessions occur.

The idea of "losing time from covering curriculum" may be distressing to some teachers. Research and teacher experience, however, clearly indicate that students and teachers gain more time than they've lost when they develop a shared vision for their work and a common set of routines that function smoothly for the rest of the year (e.g., Marzano, Marzano, & Pickering, 2003; Stronge, 2002).

Each teacher will need to decide how much time to invest in the topics suggested below and to the start-up and follow-up conversations. With students of any age, it is important to introduce ideas and routines and to review initial conversations briefly throughout the year, helping them refresh their memories about established goals and procedures, reflect on the efficacy of the goals and procedures, and refine those goals and procedures as necessary.

Regardless of grade level, there are at least six key questions that teachers need to explore with students to help develop a shared understanding of and investment in a differentiated classroom. The wording of these questions may vary according to grade, but the substance remains the same.

1. Who are you as learners? (Are you all alike or are there important differences?)

2. Given the differences we see, how should I teach you?

3. If our classroom is going to work for all of us, what will it be like? (How will it need to function? What roles will each of us play?)

4. How can I learn more about your starting points, interests, and best ways of learning?

5. If we have a differentiated classroom, can it be fair? (What will "fair" mean in this room?)

6. What will success in this class mean? (How will I know if you're succeeding? How will you know?)

Pursuit of these questions is evolutionary. In other words, each new question develops from discussions of the previous questions. For example, the fifth question about fairness only really makes sense after the first four questions are discussed. Pursuit of these questions is also recursive; teachers will need to remind students of earlier discussions with a sort of "if/then" logic as the discussions unfold. For example, "If we agree on this idea, then what will we need to do to make it work?" Finally, teachers need to revisit these questions with students at key points during the year to refresh student thinking, provide specific opportunities for students to share successes and concerns, and enable the group to contribute to a maturing of the ideas as the year progresses.

The following sections mirror the logic of these questions to help readers think about what they want their students to consider and how they might go about shaping discussions and activities to engage their students with those ideas.

Who are you as learners?

Arguably, the most important thing that any teacher of any age group in any kind of classroom does at the beginning of each year is convey a message of pleasure and excitement at the prospect of getting to know his or her students. The message has to be an honest one, of course, and when it is, it begins the long journey of building trust between teacher and learners. The message requires consistent and persistent follow-through. It needs to ring true in everything the teacher does. If trust is established between teacher and students, the latter begin to see themselves as acceptable and even valuable. They see the teacher as worthy of their trust, class content becomes more important, and learning becomes worth the risk it inevitably involves.

In a differentiated classroom, the teacher takes the message further. The message is not simply "I want to know you as people." It becomes "Knowing you individually will necessarily shape how I teach you." The implication is clear. "How could I really care to know what your strengths, needs, and interests are without wanting to act upon that knowledge in order to teach you well?"

The goals of the first conversation are to help students (1) recognize that the teacher cares about them as people and wants to know them, (2) begin to share a bit about themselves, (3) consider the similarities and differences among classmates, and (4) think about what it would mean to have a classroom designed to work for all kinds of learners. We'll present three suggestions for developing these goals with students, and we invite you to borrow one of these approaches or use them as a foundation to develop your own.

Graphing Me. Having students graph their strengths and weaknesses is an approach that is useful across many grade levels. The format can vary with the age of the students, but the goal is to have students indicate aspects of content about which they feel confident and areas in which they are less sure. Younger students might color in a premade bar graph to indicate their relative strengths and weaknesses in a variety of subject areas such as reading, art, math, writing, science, and so on. It can be useful to ask students to respond to some areas that are not directly related to school (e.g., being a friend, doing chores on time, making up games). Figure 3.1 provides an example of such a graph, and Figure 3.2 shows a graph completed by a 2nd grade student who then wrote about her graph.

Older students might follow directions and create a bar or line graph with relevant skills along the horizontal axis (e.g., computation, problem solving, fractions, equations, mathematical writing). It can be helpful to ask students to add two or three topics to the horizontal axis that do not directly relate to course content (such as hobbies or nonacademic skills) or that relate to a different course (such as math and sports skills on an English/Language Arts graph). On the vertical axis, students should place descriptors that indicate a range of performance from poor to outstanding.

To introduce this activity, it's a good idea for the teacher to complete a graph as students observe. This allows the teacher to model the assignment in a thoughtful way, it enables the teacher to introduce some ideas that may be important as the year goes on, and it allows students to get to know the teacher better. For example, the teacher may have some areas of relative weakness, areas in which his or her potential is not achieved, or an area in which he or she was once weak and perhaps even afraid but is now competent. As part of this process, we recommend that teachers create overlapping or dual graphs that illustrate growth from "then" (when the teacher was a student) to "now."

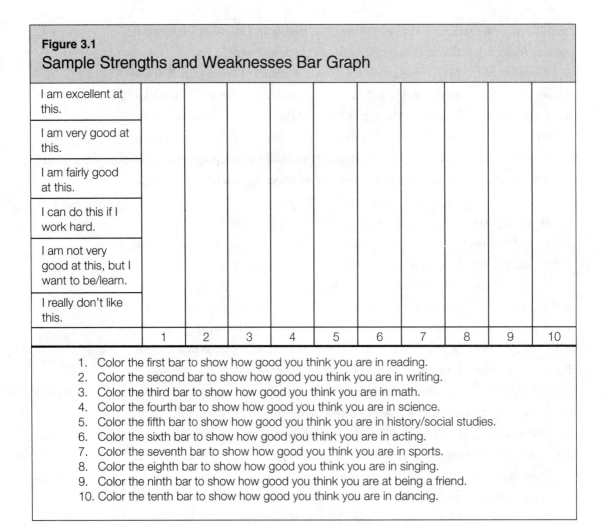

Figure 3.1

Sample Strengths and Weaknesses Bar Graph

	1	2	3	4	5	6	7	8	9	10
I am excellent at this.										
I am very good at this.										
I am fairly good at this.										
I can do this if I work hard.										
I am not very good at this, but I want to be/learn.										
I really don't like this.										

1. Color the first bar to show how good you think you are in reading.
2. Color the second bar to show how good you think you are in writing.
3. Color the third bar to show how good you think you are in math.
4. Color the fourth bar to show how good you think you are in science.
5. Color the fifth bar to show how good you think you are in history/social studies.
6. Color the sixth bar to show how good you think you are in acting.
7. Color the seventh bar to show how good you think you are in sports.
8. Color the eighth bar to show how good you think you are in singing.
9. Color the ninth bar to show how good you think you are at being a friend.
10. Color the tenth bar to show how good you think you are in dancing.

Figure 3.3 provides an example of a graph completed by a 7th grade language arts teacher for her class. The dark bars represent her proficiency when she was a young student, and the lighter bars indicate her current profile in the same area. As she creates her graph, she tells her students that she was an excellent speller when she was in elementary school, but she is now a weaker speller because she has read so many papers written by 7th graders who spell words in so many different ways. Likewise, she was a strong math student in elementary school, but she lost both skills and confidence when she began to fall behind in an 8th grade algebra class and the teacher never noticed. Her experience in that one class negatively impacted her math performance for the rest of her school years. By contrast, she explains to her students that she had always loved words and playing with words.

Figure 3.2
Mika's Strengths and Weaknesses Bar Graph

	Reading	Writing	Math	Drawing	Ballet
Excellent	▓				▓
Great	▓		▓	▓	▓
Good	▓	▓	▓	▓	▓
Fair	▓	▓	▓	▓	▓
Poor	▓	▓	▓	▓	▓

"I am excellent at reading. I am good and fair at writing. I am good and great at math and drawing. I am excellent at ballet because I've been in ballet for five years. I am worse at drawing than ballet. I am worse at writing than reading. I am better at math than writing. I am worse at writing than math. I am better at ballet than math and drawing. I am excellent at reading even though I have not done it as long as ballet."

When students complete their graphs, they should share one or two items with either the whole class (which provides a great opportunity for the teacher to observe and make notes on each student's presenting skills, speech patterns, and interests) or with a small group of peers. They can then post their graphs around the classroom, and younger students can walk around the room and look for a graph that is just like their own. It is likely that they won't find a graph that is very similar to their own, and they will certainly not find an exact duplicate. This realization readies the class for the next step in the discussion. Older students should complete the following phrase (accurately) in as many ways as possible: *In general, it's true that* _____. They will likely think of many different ways to complete the phrase, including

- In general, it's true that students in second period say they are better at interpreting lab results than students in third period say they are.
- In general, it's true that more boys say they are good at basketball.

Figure 3.3
Example of a Teacher's "Graphing Me" Graph

- In general, it's true that more students like speaking in a foreign language than reading in one.
- In general, students added topics to their graphs that they are good in, not ones they struggle to complete.

There are two observations that several students in every class nearly always make. They are particularly important to the continuing discussion.

- Nobody drew a straight line and thought they performed the same in everything.
- Everybody said they have stronger points and weaker points.

If one of these conclusions is brought up, it's time for the next step in the discussion. If no one shares either of these two conclusions, the teacher can directly prompt students with a question such as "Did anyone notice that everyone said they were better in some things and worse in others?" With these observations out in the open, the teacher can continue the discussion by saying "You know, I think about that a lot as a teacher. All of you will be better in some things and less confident in others. It's that way every year. If some of you are great with computation skills but really shaky with problem solving, and others of you are just the opposite, what should I do? How do I decide which one of you to concentrate on?"

Students typically understand the ideas behind differentiation more rapidly than teachers do. They never respond with "It doesn't matter. Don't pay attention to what we can and can't do. Just cover the material." It is likely that they will readily conclude that you should help them develop their various strengths and shore up their areas of weakness. Arriving at this sort of conclusion is the goal of this activity and its associated discussion.

There are, of course, many other ways to engage students and help them think about ways in which they differ as learners. In both of the following activities, the ultimate goal is the same as with this "Graphing Me" exercise: to draw the conclusion that student differences matter and the class will be a better one for them if the teacher teaches with those differences in mind. Regardless of which route the teacher selects to help students consider why their differences as learners are important, this is a good time to make a point that should become a classroom refrain for the remainder of the year:

> I teach because I believe every student can be successful in learning what matters. When you learn, you are stronger people. Every one of you has the potential to learn something new each and every day. The path you follow may or may not be the same as the one followed by the person sitting next to you. That's not important. What is important is that you take the next step and continue to follow your own path. My job is to work with you and make sure you continue to learn and move along that path. What I want us to figure out together during the next few days—and throughout the year—is how we can work together to create a classroom that supports every single person on their individual paths.

This is the central premise of differentiation, and it's important for students to begin to understand this core assumption.

A Trip to the Doctor. In this role play, students work with partners. In each pair, one student will play the part of a parent and the other will play the role of the parent's child (who is the same age as your students). The teacher will play the role of a physician. Directions on the cards should specify a particular medical problem that the child is experiencing such as an itchy rash, a stomach ache, an arm that was injured in a basketball game, or a headache that comes and goes. Each "child" should act in a way that's appropriate for the malady (e.g., scratching his or her rash, holding his or her stomach, cradling his or her arm, rubbing his or her forehead) while the "parent" describes the problem to the "physician." For the last two pairs, the role play cards should indicate that the parent introduces the problem to the doctor and then says, "My son/daughter will tell you about it." The students playing the sick children then speak for themselves. Figure 3.4 shows examples of two role play cards.

Figure 3.4
Sample Role Play Cards

ROLE PLAY INSTRUCTIONS

Scenario:
You will play the role of a parent. Your partner will play the role of your son/daughter. The teacher will play the role of a physician.

Your child is not feeling well because of an itchy and painful rash, so you're at the doctor's office to see if you can get some help for the rash.

Here's what you should do:
Greet the doctor and explain that your son/daughter has a really bad rash on his/her arms. Tell the doctor that it started over the weekend after you returned from your parents' house. Explain that you think the rash may be poison ivy because your child and his/her grandfather worked outside a lot, but mention that you're not sure because your child is often in the outdoors and has never had poison ivy. Ask for a prescription to help with the itching and pain.

Here's what your partner will do:
He/She will act like he/she is very uncomfortable and scratch his/her arms every once in a while. After the doctor says to not scratch the rash, he/she will just hold or rub his/her arms a little.

Here's what both of you should do:
When the doctor gives the diagnosis and prescription, react appropriately and leave the doctor's office (go back to your seats).

ROLE PLAY INSTRUCTIONS

Scenario:
Your partner will play the role of your parent. You will play the role of the son/daughter. The teacher will play the role of a physician.

You are not feeling well because of possible broken arm, so you're at the doctor's office to see if you can get some help.

Here's what you should do:
Act like you feel really uncomfortable. Hold your arm like you're trying to protect it.

Here's what your partner will do:
He/She will greet the doctor and explain that you hurt your arm in a basketball game last night. He/She thought it was just a sprain, but the pain got worse all night long and now you can't move your arm. He/She is worried that it might be broken and needs the doctor's help.

Here's what both of you should do:
When the doctor gives the diagnosis and prescription, react appropriately and leave the doctor's office (go back to your seats).

The last pair of students to participate should role play a common cold. In all cases (regardless of the actual illness), the physician should listen attentively and then say, "I'm so sorry you're not feeling well. Here's some cold medicine. Take it and see if it helps." By the time the last pair gets to the doctor, the students are generally relieved to find that someone actually has symptoms that match the remedy. The teacher might want to ask, "How many times would you or your parents visit that doctor before you or they decided she wasn't very good and you didn't want to go back?"

At some point, it's also good to ask, "Why do you think the adults always talked for their children? At the end, when the students finally spoke up for themselves, rather than relying on their parents to speak for them, did they explain the problem well enough for you to get what was wrong?" This sidebar can help introduce the idea that students often know what they need as well as, or better than, adults do and that they should freely say whenever they see a way to make the class better for them.

All that's necessary for students to get the point of this role play is for the teacher to ask, "Why did we just do that? What's it got to do with school?" Students usually respond that it's no more effective in school for a teacher to do the same thing with everyone, no matter their need, than for the doctor to prescribe the same thing to every patient, no matter the symptom. This, again, positions the teacher to say, "I think teachers are like doctors because they should understand their students' various needs and prescribe what is necessary to help the particular student function well. Do you agree?"

One Size Fits All? A third activity that helps students begin to think about classrooms that attend to students' varying needs starts with the teacher asking two students to put on jackets that are clearly the wrong size for them. The teacher selects two students who are very different in height and stature, but he or she should make sure the students are comfortable in front of the class (or being the center of attention). The smaller student should put on a jacket that is several sizes too large for him or her. After students have had a few moments to giggle, the larger student should attempt to put on a jacket that is several sizes too small for him or her.

The two students then describe how they feel in the clothes. Answers are often lighthearted and a little silly. The teacher should allow for a slight pause to consider the answers before asking them to describe how they think they'd feel at the end of the day if they had to wear the jackets all day long. Students typically begin to see potential problems that are a little more serious (e.g., "I'd have trouble eating lunch because the sleeves would get in my food," or "I don't think I could write very well because it's hard to move my arms.") Finally, the teacher should ask them to describe what they think would happen if they had to wear clothes of this size all year. Generally, students easily see that what initially seemed silly, unimportant, or slightly inconvenient could become a serious impediment to doing what they like to do (e.g., "I think I'd begin to see myself as a slob," or "I don't know if kids would want me to work with them in school because I couldn't do much to help with projects since I can hardly move.")

Once again, it's generally only necessary to ask the class, "Why do you think we just did this? What's it got to do with school or with this class?" Students will often talk about how uncomfortable it is when class activities or assignments are the "wrong size" and it becomes difficult to do the work. They sometimes share examples from their own school experiences when work seemed to always be "too big" or "too small" for them, and they are generally quite able to explain both short-term and long-term fallout from those experiences.

As is the case with the previous two examples, this activity easily leads to the conclusion, "When you look around the room, it's clear that not everyone wears the same size clothes. My experience as a teacher has shown me just as clearly that identical tasks won't always be a good fit for everyone in the classroom either. What do you think a teacher should do about the fact that not all students are exactly alike in their needs at a particular time?" With this in mind, students should be ready to move to the next step in the discussion.

Given the differences we see, how should I teach you?

Whether the teacher elects to use one of the three activities explained above or develop another approach, it is important for students to acknowledge that people don't come in matched sets like luggage. Human differences are not only normal, they are valuable. If we were all clones of one another, the world would be much less interesting and people would be much less prepared to address the issues and problems that are inevitable in life. We'd exhibit very limited creativity.

In this portion of the conversation, the teacher should pose some questions that are specific to his or her grade and subject level for students to consider. Examples include

- Let's say there are some students in our physics class who are very strong in science but haven't had chemistry yet. Would you expect any important learner needs to arise that are specific to this group of students? What should I do about them?

• What if we have some students in our class who have no trouble memorizing spelling words—and we have some other students who always find spelling to be the hardest thing they do? Does it make sense that both groups of students should always have exactly the same spelling words? Would they all learn equally well?

• What if we have some students in our class who are happiest and most productive when they work in groups—and we have others who much prefer to learn alone? Whose preference should I honor when I'm trying to decide how to set up the class for the work we need to accomplish?

• Suppose we have some students in our Spanish class who have a great ear for language. They can repeat almost everything they hear me say, and they do it accurately. On the other hand, writing in Spanish is a chore for them. No matter how hard they work, they can't seem to write as quickly, or as accurately, as some other students. Likewise, suppose we have some students who write in Spanish easily, but they get knots in their stomach when they have to speak in class. Does any of that matter? Is there a way I could be a better teacher for all students? Is there a way that we could set up the class to work better for everyone's unique needs?

As the class discusses particular scenarios, students work together to name specific ways in which they could be more flexible so more of their classmates get what they need to succeed. Examples include

• It might be better if students could choose books to read that they are interested in.

• Some students might already know a lot about what we're getting ready to study, and it would be better for them to do work that is new and challenging for them.

• It might be better if we had a choice of ways to show what we are learning. Some students might want to write about it, but others might do a better job of making a chart or doing a demonstration.

• It might help if we could work with friends to learn something or get help when we don't understand something. Some students might do better trying to figure out an idea alone, or they could work with the teacher to get unstuck.

- Some of us might need longer to work on something in order to get it done right.

- Some of us might want to work longer on something because we like it a lot and want to learn more about it.

- Some of us might learn better if the teacher uses demonstrations and examples instead of only lecturing.

- Some of us might learn better if we get to try out an idea instead of just hearing about it.

The point of this segment of the shared conversation is for students to begin to imagine and articulate some ways in which they might learn better if the classroom provided more options. It's good for as many ideas as possible to come from the students, but it's also effective for the teacher to offer some ideas for consideration.

Pause every so often to ask questions such as "How do these ideas sound to you? What sounds positive about them, and what are some concerns you have?" It's not necessary to address particular concerns at this point, but it might be wise to list them for future discussions as the conversation moves ahead.

If our classroom is going to work for all of us, what will it be like?

At this stage, students need to begin to work with the teacher to move from an idea to a practical reality. In other words, it's now important to talk about (1) what the classroom might look like and (2) what role each person will need to play (as well as what they shouldn't do) in order to contribute to the success of the classroom. Again, appropriate language and length of time spent on any segment of the conversation will vary with students' ages, the teacher's goals, and the context of the class. In all cases, however, the goal is to set early expectations for classroom operation and establish shared responsibility for its success.

A number of these elements will be discussed in greater detail in Part II of this book. Here, however, we'll propose some of the big ideas or principles that make a flexible classroom work. The goal is to help students think about and contribute to basic elements that are useful in a flexible classroom and help students learn as much and as efficiently as possible. This includes, but is not limited to, opportunities for each student to

- Use materials that are a good fit.
- Connect important ideas to personal interests.

- Work with knowledge and skills that are at the next step in growth.
- Work at a pace that supports learning.
- Receive help from the teacher and peers that support growth and success.
- Explore ideas and skills in ways that are effective and efficient.
- Express learning in ways that show what he or she has learned.
- Learn with and from a variety of classmates.
- Teach a variety of classmates.
- Learn how to be a more independent learner.
- Learn how to be a better group member and partner.

A classroom in which these opportunities are available (when appropriate) suggests a setting in which

- Students sometimes work alone and sometimes in small groups of peers.
- Students sometimes work with the teacher as a whole class and sometimes individually or in small groups.
- Students have access to many kinds of materials that support learning, including multiple sets of reading materials, Internet resources, and video and audio resources.
- Room arrangements are flexible—furniture can be rearranged depending on need.
- Students are able to finish their work at different times.
- Students sometimes have different in-class assignments.
- Students sometimes have different homework assignments.
- The teacher sometimes works with individuals or small groups while the rest of the class works independently or in small groups.

If there are particular elements that the teacher feels should be implemented early in the school year, then it's important to make sure those elements are part of the discussion. If students raise possibilities that seem to suggest more than the teacher feels is manageable early in the year, then it's a good idea to keep a running list (perhaps on chart paper so students can see their ideas recorded and return to them when they need to), which will grow as the year progresses as students continue to think of and add new ideas and routines. Note that as everyone begins to work with the ideas, it will no doubt be necessary to fine tune the ideas.

Once students and the teacher have proposed a fundamental set of elements that are essential to a differentiated, flexible, or responsive classroom, it's time to consider the implications of those elements for everyone involved. The teacher might begin this consideration by saying, "Let's take a closer look at a few of the ideas we have raised and talk about what each person in the class will need to do, or avoid doing, so that the ideas can work well for everyone. This should help us get started smoothly as we begin our work this year."

In the beginning, present the elements that are critical to implementing differentiation, are fundamental to operating a flexible classroom, and raise the points with which you will need the greatest amount of student understanding and cooperation. Figure 3.5 suggests some of these elements and some of the implications for both the teacher and students.

While the particulars will vary among classrooms, the discussion this activity sparks should help students begin to understand *why* they will be asked to do certain things, not do others, and work in specific ways. More students will work more effectively from a shared rationale or vision than from a static set of abstract rules posted on the wall.

How can I learn more about your starting points, interests, and best ways of learning?

Clearly, differentiation is based on acceptance of the reality that learning is shaped by a variety of factors, including prior experiences, culture, economics, language, interests, learning preferences, and support systems. To teach a student well, a teacher must know that student well. That is a formidable charge, and the truth is that no teacher will ever know his or her students deeply. However, this should not suggest that it is impossible for a teacher to learn systematically about students at a level that supports differentiated, personalized, or responsive teaching.

Over time, a teacher should aspire to know some general things, such as how well his or her students read, what they like to do with their spare time, what their dreams are, how they relate to their peers, how they see themselves as learners, how they learn best, and how their culture shapes their learning. As various aspects of the curriculum unfold, the teacher needs to know whether students bring with them prerequisite knowledge and skills, what they understand and misunderstand, the degree to which they have mastered or surpassed expectations at a given time, which instructional approaches work well for them and which do not, and whether they can connect key ideas to their personal lives and experiences.

Figure 3.5
Critical Elements in a Differentiated Classroom and Their Implications

Goal/Element in a Flexible Classroom	Implications for the Teacher	Implications for Students
Students need to	*The teacher*	*Students*
Work in small groups with classmates.	• Will ensure that all groups have assignments that work for the group so everyone can learn what they need to learn. • Will ensure that each group has clear directions. • Will ensure that students know how to work together effectively. • Will provide directions for moving furniture to allow for a variety of groupings.	• Will focus on what their group should do rather than pay attention to what others are doing. • Will ensure that they understand the directions given to their group and follow them. • Will contribute to the effectiveness of their group and ask for help when there is a problem the group can't solve. • Will monitor their conversations so noise doesn't detract from learning. • Will move furniture smoothly so groups have appropriate spaces to work.
Work with the teacher individually or in small groups.	• Will know what each student requires in order to learn at a given time so the groups support learning. • Will ensure that student directions are clear and that students have ways to get help when he or she is busy with a small group or individual. • Will keep track of student needs, work, and growth and help students do the same for themselves.	• Will be able to start and stop individual and small-group work efficiently to meet with the teacher when necessary. • Will not interrupt the teacher when he or she is working with individuals or groups. • Will know how to get help when the teacher is busy with groups or individuals. • Will keep track of their own learning goals and work.
Spend different amounts of time on a task in order to learn well.	• Will provide a place for students to turn in completed work and get it checked if necessary. • Will provide options for important student work when a task is finished (i.e., anchor activities).	• Will follow directions about turning in work or getting it checked when it's finished. • Will work with anchor activities smoothly and effectively when an assignment is completed.
Work with different materials in order to learn well.	• Will provide a variety of materials that work for students' different entry points, including reading needs, interests, and formats. • Will help develop a way to make sure students know which materials to use at a particular time and where materials will be stored.	• Will help make sure materials are cared for and returned to the place they belong after an activity is completed. • Will help the teacher know which materials (or kinds of materials) work best for them as individuals.

In an effectively differentiated classroom, ongoing assessment informs every important instructional decision a teacher makes. Early in the year, students need to know that their teacher is also a student who diligently studies two things—the content he or she teaches and the students themselves. This message needs to be clear from the first day of school and evident every day that follows. At some point in the early conversations about creating a classroom that supports each student's success, it is important for students to hear the following:

- I want to know you as a person because you're interesting to me.
- I need to know you as a student so that I can determine what your next steps in learning are.
- I will watch you as you work in class as closely as I can because what I learn will help me plan better for you individually and for the class as a whole.
- You'll see me take notes while you work and while we discuss things in class. This helps me learn more about how learning works for you.
- In the first few days of school, I'll ask you to do some things that will give me a reasonable sense of your starting points this year and about who you are as a learner.
- Throughout the year, I'll often ask you to share what you're learning so I can help you take your next step as a learner.
- Much of the time, I'll be less interested in grading your work and more interested in giving you information that will help you learn better and increase your chances of success when I do grade your work.
- I'll often invite you to tell me how you're feeling about your work and what is going well or poorly for you in class. I hope you'll always feel free to honestly tell me those things, even if I forget to ask.

Depending on the age of the students and the nature of the class, students might be prompted to express what they wish their teachers knew about them, how they think teachers could use what they learn about students in order to teach better, or how teachers might get to know them better and faster. This element of the conversation, however, is to tell students that they will mutually create the teacher's role in the classroom: to continually learn about the students so he or she can be a more effective teacher for each of them. It also lets students know that an assessment of their strengths, needs, and interests will begin almost immediately. Students, too, need to begin to understand that teaching and learning work better when everyone knows what the learning targets are, when the teacher and a particular student know where that student is in relation to the target at a given time, and when both use that information to move ahead.

If we have a differentiated classroom, can it be fair?

While the four questions posed prior to this one should generally be pursued with students during the first few days of school, the question of "fairness" is probably best introduced after the class has begun to work in a differentiated setting and after routines to support differentiation are largely in place. In other words, the first significant conversation about fairness should take place after students have enough experience in a differentiated classroom to understand its rationale and to have experienced how it works for them as individuals and as a group. Depending on the particular setting, that might mean at the end of the first month of school—or a little later.

The teacher might begin the conversation by reviewing some of the goals, procedures, and routines that the group previously discussed and are now in place. He or she might then say something like, "It's been useful to me to hear your ideas about these things as we've begun to create our classroom. I have an additional question I'd like to get your thinking on today. It's often the case that people say a classroom is fair when everyone does everything alike—or when a teacher makes sure everyone gets exactly the same work and materials and time allotments for work. As we've agreed, however, it's not always best for everyone to do everything alike. Does that make our classroom unfair? What do you think 'fair' means in this classroom?"

Student responses will vary for a range of reasons. Often, however, early in the year, students in differentiated classroom will suggest that the class is fair if the teacher seems to like everyone alike, or if he or she doesn't seem to have favorites. Sometimes, students will say the class is fair if the teacher pays about the same amount of attention to everyone.

Over time, if a differentiated classroom is working as it should, students will generally conclude that the class is fair if everyone gets what they need in order to succeed. The shift from "fair = identical treatment" to "fair = equity of opportunity to grow and succeed" is an important one because it embodies the nature and intent of differentiation. In addition, if students have difficulty shifting from more traditional definitions of "fairness" to a perspective supported by differentiation, it's important for the teacher to be aware of that and understand what obstacles stand in the way of the class feeling fair to its members. This part of the conversation is worth exploring relatively early in the year and revisiting as the year evolves.

What will success in this class mean?

One of the seemingly immutable artifacts of "how we do school" is that success is typically defined in terms of a grade on a report card. Not only is that a *limited* view of success, it's a *limiting* one as well. There are students who make steady *As* on report cards with little effort or evidence of growth, and there are students who make low grades but have every right to cheer because they have demonstrated heroic commitment to learning and have grown remarkably despite falling short of a specified goal.

We'll discuss grading in differentiated classrooms in more detail later in this book. However, at some point relatively early in the year, it's important for the teacher to involve students in thinking about what it means to be successful in life—and in the classroom. This might be done by presenting students with brief biographies of two famous figures, one of whom gets lots of attention but makes little substantial contribution to anything worthwhile and one of whom devotes more attention to making a difference than to being in the spotlight. It might be done by having students compare two characters in a book or movie, one of whom has a harder life than the other but continues to work toward a goal in spite of the difficulties. It might be done through an example of two (unidentifiable) students—one in whom the teacher feels great pride despite the fact that the other student receives more accolades. It might be accomplished by sharing personal stories about times when students felt genuinely proud of themselves and other times when they knew they had little to be proud of in spite of praise from others. The point of this discussion is to raise the possibility that rewards—grades included—don't often reveal the whole story.

This is also a time to let students know that they are encouraged to think about success as having several parts. One is how hard a person works in order to grow. A second is how much a person grows. The third is whether a person reaches or exceeds a goal that required growth. Teachers should help students begin to develop and consider language that reflects these three markers of success. Students should also be assured that the teacher will be looking for attributes such as the following and will ask them to also look for these attributes in themselves.

- Hard work.
- Personal goals that require constant work and attention.

- Willingness to take intellectual risks (i.e., to take a chance when something seems hard to do).
- Willingness to revise work to make it better.
- Willingness to seek help in order to grow and succeed with difficult tasks.
- Significant progress and substantial growth.
- Persistence in reaching or surpassing class goals.

Two principles that benefit learners and learning are that (1) working diligently and intelligently leads to growth and (2) growth ultimately enables individuals to achieve and exceed most goals. This is the essence of a growth mind-set—a fundamental underpinning of differentiation—and it is essential for genuine success. We fare best in the long term when we compete against ourselves rather than against other people.

Let students know that they will often hear you ask, "Is this the best *you* can do—the most *you* can give to this task?" Let them know that you hope they will join you in celebrating growth whenever it occurs for any student in the classroom.

None of the six questions explored in this chapter should be seen as "handled" during a single conversation. Teachers who lead students to develop a shared classroom vision that seeks to maximize growth for every student will help students continue to explore the questions and their relevance throughout the year. Subsequent conversations may be short or long, individual or group, but they will be necessary for ideas about the classroom to "grow up" as the year progresses.

Teachers as Leaders of Parents in Understanding Differentiation

There are at least three important points to make about teachers who work effectively with parents to help them understand and contribute to a class that is focused on the success of each individual learner. First, it is important for teachers to realize the important role parents can play in helping a teacher know the students better. Parents will always have greater depth of knowledge about their children than a teacher can ever hope to attain. On the other hand, teachers (at least after a few years in the classroom) have much greater breadth of knowledge about students of a particular age and in a particular subject than most parents can ever hope to attain. A wise teacher invites parents to contribute their depth of knowledge and, in turn, offers those parents a perspective on their children that is derived from a broad awareness of the childhood development. It is a much better idea to proactively forge a mutually beneficial partnership than to allow an adversarial relationship to develop with parents. A teacher in a differentiated classroom simply needs help to know each student better, and most parents are a fantastic source of that information.

Second, it is critical for teachers to understand the role that culture plays in shaping parental response to school. This is particularly critical if parents are not from the majority culture. For example, parents from some cultural groups may feel uncomfortable if they think that they are being asked to tell the teacher how to do his or her job; they consider it disrespectful of the teacher's competence. Parents from cultures that operate from a collectivistic (as opposed to an individualistic) perspective may be uncomfortable if their child seems singled out for praise because their culture emphasizes the group over the individual. For the same reason, parents from collectivistic cultures may initially be more interested in hearing about their child's behavior in and contribution to the group than about grades and test scores (Rothstein-Fisch & Trumbull, 2008). It is also extremely important to know that parents from all backgrounds care about and want to support the success of their children. Absence from parent meetings may have much more to do with a lack of transportation, child care, or confidence with English than with personal attitudes about the importance of school. Teachers who are culturally competent invest in understanding the diverse cultures of their students, and they use that knowledge to build successful partnerships with both children and their parents.

Third, few parents argue with the baseline intent of differentiation if it is articulated clearly and in a way that is relevant to their desires and concerns. The fundamental message about differentiation from a teacher to a parent should be

- I am pleased that I will be teaching your child this year and want to do everything I can to make it a successful year for him/her.
- I have learned over the years that I am a better teacher when I understand my students' particular strengths and needs as individual learners.
- I want to know what you value for your son/daughter this year so that I can support him/her in developing in those areas.
- I hope you will help me understand what some of your child's strengths and needs are as the year continues.

- My intent in class is to use what I can learn to help your child grow as much and as fast as possible to achieve and, in some cases, exceed the goals that are established for our class.

There are few parents who would respond, "I don't want you to know my kid, and I don't want you to help him learn as much as possible." What the philosophy and practice of differentiation aims to do is precisely what most parents want for their children—a class in which a student is known and valued as an individual and where there is a reliable support system to build on the student's strengths, help shore up or circumvent weaknesses, and maximize academic growth for the time that the student is a member of the class.

Teachers can do the same activity with parents at a back-to-school night that they used to introduce differentiation to their students. As the year progresses, they should take every opportunity to communicate clearly and without educational jargon that they are (1) working diligently to set clear goals for the class, (2) persistently following the progress of their students with regard to the goals, (3) providing clear feedback to the students to help them grow, and (4) using what they learn about students and their development to help them grow as far and as fast as possible. At every opportunity, teachers should also invite parents to share insights that will help them do their job better.

Be sure, however, that the emperor is wearing clothes. In other words, deliver what you promise. If a student is having difficulty reading or writing in 10th grade, do what's necessary to support the student's growth in that area—even if you are a math or science teacher. If you have a 3rd grader who has mastered 6th grade math, do what's necessary to help the student grow mathematically—even if that means you have to find new collaborators or learn more math. If we want parents to trust us, we have to earn their trust.

Teachers as Leaders of Colleagues in Understanding Differentiation

Teachers who lead for differentiation have an opportunity to lead colleagues, including other teachers and principals, as well as students and their parents. Accepting this opportunity can benefit both the teacher leader and his or her colleagues. Teachers have been criticized for engaging in "private practice"—for staying to ourselves, for not sharing our practice with other teachers, and for failing to learn from other teachers. Teacher leaders who share their work with differentiation take care not to convey the message that they are resident experts or that they have completed their learning about differentiation. Rather, the message is that the teacher is interested in sharing ideas with colleagues who will help them grow in their work. When you lead peers to an understanding of and contribution to differentiation, the potential opportunities and benefits are limitless. Consider the following:

- Coplanning or coteaching with specialists (e.g., English language learner (ELL), special education, reading, gifted education, media, technology specialists) enriches the teacher's repertoire, extends learning support for his or her students, integrates specialties into the regular classroom, and helps to forge teams that work across specialties on behalf of a wide range of students.

- Inviting colleagues to be a "second pair of hands" on occasions when another adult is needed can provide necessary images of flexible teaching and learning for teachers who may want to address student variance but don't know how to begin.

- Working with colleagues to develop and share relevant knowledge about students' cultures and using that knowledge in instructional planning can help incorporate more cultural awareness into all classrooms.

- Planning differentiated lessons with grade-level or subject-matter peers is much more efficient than "every-man-for-himself" planning. It also allows teachers to contribute to their areas of greatest strength while they learn from others who have different strengths.

- Sharing pertinent insights about students with their teachers for the following year can give those teachers a more informed start and help them maintain a link with the previous teachers.

- Debating the merits of differentiation with other teachers can sharpen understanding and practice on both sides.

- Sharing ideas for differentiation with peers who want to address learner needs is both a gift and a relevant form of professional development.

- Providing staff development for peers can mute the voices that say, "Not in this school, not with these students." It can also show teachers how to begin addressing student variance, explain how to avoid pitfalls, and send the clear message that even teachers who seem ahead of the game still have room to grow.

If schools reflected a perfect world, every principal would be an informed advocate and supporter of classrooms that address the range of needs for every learner. Unfortunately, schools do not reflect (and are not in themselves) a perfect world. Principals work from the same limited understandings and conceptions of differentiation that virtually all other educators do, and many principals (and other administrative leaders) find it difficult to stay abreast of contemporary pedagogy. Even many principals who have a fundamental understanding of differentiation, and a sense that it's important to attend to students' varied learning needs, may lack the appropriate depth of understanding and experience necessary to provide effective guidance to teachers.

A teacher who is willing to be a leader of principals, supervisors, or other administrators has the opportunity to benefit not only those individuals, but also those colleagues who are affected by their practice. Consider the following insights that might result from conversations with or visits to the classroom of a teacher who is effectively differentiating instruction—insights that correct common misconceptions some administrators and supervisors have about differentiation.

- Students in a flexible classroom are focused on their work. Movement and conversation are purposeful. The classroom is not disorderly.
- Students who are disengaged in other settings work with concentration in this class.
- Students have a greater level of independence and awareness about their work than in many other settings. When work is a good fit for students, discipline improves.
- Differentiation doesn't happen all day, every day, but it occurs when a teacher learns through observation and assessment about particular student needs.
- Student groups in a differentiated classroom should be flexible, changing many times each day or week.
- In a differentiated class, students often use different paths to achieve common goals.

By inviting principals and other administrative leaders to observe and discuss differentiation, a teacher leader is likely to gain more support for his or her work while extending the capacity of the administrator to support the work of other teachers in a more knowledgeable manner. In addition, of course, the questions and insights of an educator whose view of the classroom is somewhat different from that of the teacher's can stretch the teacher's thinking about differentiation as well.

Michael Fullan reminds us that strong leaders challenge us to look for solutions to challenges that have no easy answers (2001a). It is certainly the case that preparing an increasingly diverse student population to function with confidence at a high level in an increasingly complex world is just such a challenge. A teacher who leads for differentiation lives daily with that challenge, and he or she engages students, colleagues, and superordinates in confronting that challenge, asking the uncomfortable questions that necessarily surround it, and joining perspectives to find better solutions. Everyone benefits.

Part II of this book will address the more "practical" aspects of leading and managing for differentiation. It will examine some key aspects of what teachers in effectively differentiated classrooms *do* in order to enact what they *believe.*

Part II

Managing a
Differentiated Classroom

Contrary to common misperceptions, classroom management is not simply the process of arranging desks, rewarding good behavior, and choosing consequences for misconduct. Classroom management encompasses many practices integral to teaching, such as developing relationships; structuring classroom communities where students can work productively; organizing productive work around meaningful curriculum; teaching moral development and citizenship; making decisions about timing and other aspects of instructional planning; successfully motivating students to learn; and encouraging parent involvement.

—Pamela LePage, Linda Darling-Hammond, & Hanife Akar,
Preparing Teachers for a Changing World

The students are in place. The teacher has the desire to know and teach them as individuals, and he or she has a solid understanding of what high-quality differentiation is and why implementing differentiation improves the prospects of his or her students. The teacher is developing or fine tuning meaningful learning outcomes, devising assessments that align with those outcomes, and creating daily lesson plans designed to move students systematically to proficiency with those goals (Erickson, 2006; Tomlinson et al., 2009; Wiggins & McTighe, 2005). The teacher is also working to integrate differentiation into his or her design for high-quality curriculum (Tomlinson & McTighe, 2006), has preliminary plans for how to differentiate effectively (Tomlinson, 1999, 2001, 2004), and has begun to issue an invitation to students to help create a classroom that is designed to work for each of them.

This sounds like a great start, and it is. However, it's only a start. Even with these elements in working order and guided by a productively evolving philosophy, there's at least one more piece to the puzzle.

A teacher who has the best intentions, dynamic curriculum, and plans for differentiation cannot—and will not—move forward unless that teacher is at ease with translating the ideas into classroom practice. In other words, teachers who are uncomfortable with flexible classroom management will *not* differentiate instruction, even if they understand it, accept the need for it, and can plan for it (Brighton et al., 2005). The chapters that follow in Part II are intended to support teachers as they develop and extend their comfort level in this area. Part II, then, deals with the nuts and bolts of managing a student-centered classroom, which, by its nature, requires flexible use of virtually every classroom element. This is a good place to distinguish again between classroom *management* and classroom *leadership*.

A teacher can manage a flexible schedule, places to keep supplies, labels that help students know which materials to access, a schedule for small-group instruction, ways to curb the noise that is a part of collaborative student work, and so on. However, he or she must lead students to understand and contribute to a differentiated classroom, overcome their fear of failure or challenge, invest in their own success, and cooperate with the routines that constitute classroom management. A teacher can manage these details without much of a philosophy. Real leadership, then, requires an ethical compass regarding the responsibility of leadership, the value of those whom the leader asks to trust him or her, and the worthiness of the destination toward which the leader guides the group.

In the chapters ahead, we'll describe many ways to proactively plan for potential "hot spots" in differentiated classrooms in order to develop a setting in which the teacher and students can work together to the benefit of each learner.

Remember, too, that enlisting the trust of young people to be full participants in a differentiated classroom is a matter of leadership.

As you read Part II of this book, ask yourself often how the concrete ideas that are presented will be shaped by your understanding of differentiation, your philosophy of teaching, and the degree to which you are able to share those underpinnings with your students. In other words, continue to think about the ways in which effective leadership and management are interdependent.

4

Learning Environment
Setting the Stage for Academic Success

Learning occurs best in a positive environment—one that contains positive interpersonal relationships and interactions, that contains comfort and order, and in which the learner feels appreciated, acknowledged, respected, and validated.

—Barbara McCombs and Jo Sue Whisler,
The Learner-Centered Classroom and School

Few teachers argue with propositions that some students

- Require more time than others to achieve particular understandings or to master particular skills.
- Bring with them to the classroom great reservoirs of knowledge that other students do not bring.
- Need to move around more than others.

- Seem to have given up on school—or on themselves or adults—and are angry or lethargic much of the time.
- Have difficulty concentrating during whole-class discussions and perform much better in small-group instruction.
- Are poor test takers but actually understand the content of the curriculum.
- Will not engage with learning if they fail to see the point of it.

Therefore, the question is not whether teachers recognize that such differences exist in virtually every classroom, or even whether they impact student success. The question that plagues teachers is how to attend to the evident differences in a room that contains so many young bodies.

The purpose of developing a differentiated classroom is to make sure that there's opportunity and support for each student to learn essential knowledge and skills as effectively and efficiently as possible. In other words, differentiation exists to "make room" for all kinds of learners to succeed academically. It also "makes room" for the teacher to support academic success with the freedom to tailor instruction for each student. Central to this process of "making room" for responsive teaching and student-focused learning is the creation of a learning environment that invites flexibility—in other words, a classroom where flexibility is the norm.

In fact, a flexible classroom is important to learning in general, not just to differentiation. Experts tell us that there are three categories of classrooms in terms of classroom management: *dysfunctional, adequate,* and *orderly.*

- *Dysfunctional* classroom environments are, of course, often chaotic. The teacher consistently struggles to maintain "control." Little sustained learning can take place.
- *Adequate* classroom environments exhibit a basic level of order, but the teacher still struggles to maintain it. Some learning takes place some of the time.
- *Orderly* classroom environments fall into two further categories—*restrictive* and *enabling* environments.
- Orderly, *restrictive* learning environments are "tight-ship" classrooms. The teacher maintains a high degree of structure, manages routines tightly, and uses few instructional strategies.
- Orderly, *enabling* learning environments are found in smoothly running classrooms that manifest a looser (but not loose) structure. In these

classrooms, teachers use a wide range of routines and instructional strategies, and the emphasis is on students making meaning of content. (Educational Research Service, 1993)

In fact, researchers tell us, there is a direct relationship between a teacher's ability to manage a complex set of activities in a classroom and his or her ability to teach intellectually challenging material (LePage, Darling-Hammond, & Akar, 2005). This is because tasks that require comprehension and problem solving require more flexibility than rote learning. When teachers are afraid of what might happen when students work independently, in small groups, with inquiry-oriented tasks, or at varied paces, they often opt to use more passive approaches to learning that effectually "dumb down" the curriculum. In those instances, teachers lower their expectations for students by using simpler modes of presentation and evaluation as a trade-off for classroom order. In other words, in those circumstances, teachers "teach defensively."

There are some sad and predictable cycles perpetuated by educators' perceptions that most students can only function maturely in tight-ship classrooms. One of those cycles stems from the reality that students often misbehave when the work they are asked to do is consistently too hard or too easy for them. Teachers in dysfunctional and adequate classrooms, as well as many who believe in the tight-ship model, necessarily persist in giving students tasks that are a poor fit for some of them (because differentiating requires flexibility, which threatens order). In turn, some students continue to be frustrated (and show it), which further reinforces the teacher's perception that to "loosen the reins" would be catastrophic. This conclusion, of course, simply feeds the frustration of many young people.

A second regrettable cycle is an artifact from tracking practices in many of our schools. It is easy for educators to associate student behavior with student ability. Unfortunately, students who misbehave are rarely seen as very bright (even when they are). Many teachers have grown comfortable with separating out students by "ability" and then teaching them in various tracks according to what "they can handle." Students who are frustrated by this mismatch, and who predictably act out as a result, are often placed in low-track classes (typified by low-level curriculum) that are run as tight ships or are either dysfunctional or adequate in terms of management. Conversely, students who comply with teacher directives are more likely to be seen as bright, and they are taught in orderly, flexible settings—that is, in classrooms where the emphasis is on comprehension and where teachers readily use a wide variety of instructional strategies to engage students with important ideas and skills (Carbonaro & Gamoran, 2002; Gamoran et al., 1995; Haberman, 1991; Hodges, 2001).

Differentiation advocates teaching each student as an individual worthy and capable of handling a meaning-rich curriculum. It also advocates an environment in which each student comes to understand, own, and value his or her capacity as a learner. Doing so requires an orderly, flexible classroom environment. This chapter will focus on some key elements, guidelines, and strategies that create just such an environment.

Staging a Successful Drama

Think for a bit about a stage performance and the role of a good director. Clearly, successful directors don't simply buy scripts, put them in the hands of actors, give a few directions, and expect compelling results. In fact, much of the power behind a play that "works" happens *around* rather than *in* the script. Along the way, a successful director must create affective and physical environments in which the play will evolve.

En route to creating a play that works for an audience, the director has to make it work for the actors. This happens on at least two levels. First, the director has to come to know and understand each actor as an individual—his or her strengths and vulnerabilities, preferred ways of working, and life experiences. It is upon these individual aspects that the director will draw as rehearsals progress. Not knowing these things would not only limit the potential impact of the actor, but of the director as well. To prepare, the director will likely do some background "research" on the actor before rehearsals begin. This will be followed by individual conversations throughout the rehearsal cycle, and by careful observation and reflection to understand what makes the actor shine as a character in some instances and what makes it difficult for the actor to bring a character to life in others.

In addition to learning to know and understand the actors as individuals, the director needs to help the actors move from being a collection of individuals to a cast, a troupe, an ensemble, a company—a team. They need to unify around a shared and commonly understood endeavor, without losing their distinctiveness. In other words, the director has to help build a sense of community among the actors so that the group works cohesively to benefit both individual and shared development. If the director is successful, the actors will develop valuable bonds during the production cycle. They will learn to pull together, support one another, cover for one another's shortcomings, and ultimately leave one another with both gratitude and sadness. Each individual will be stronger because of the group. The group will be stronger because of the individuals. Therefore, the director begins building an ensemble from disparate individuals when the actors arrive on day one—if not before. This work continues until the final curtain comes down.

Finally, in building an environment in which the actors can evolve, the director must create a physical context for the play. In the theater, of course, this is called a set. It is a miniature world designed on a small piece of real estate called a stage. It will contain whatever is necessary to make the play come to life and enhance the work of the actors. Nothing on the set is without purpose. From flats to props, everything contributes to the viability of the little universe. Shape, color, design, texture, and location are elements that sculpt the play and enliven the acting. When the set is ready, it is almost never final. Changes are nearly always made right up until opening night, and they will often continue throughout the life of the play.

The role of the teacher in developing an effective classroom environment is much like the role of the director. The drama, of course, is a compelling one—the interaction of individuals with ideas and skills that will change the individuals for better or worse. It requires risk, extreme effort, failure, self-awareness, honesty, small victories, and major triumphs. To make the drama work, the teacher must work quickly to get to know the actors and persistently understand them. He or she must begin early to build a team from a group of disparate individuals and continue the team-building process for as long as the drama runs. In a small piece of real estate called a classroom, the teacher must offer a set in which the actors can work to make the play compelling. The remainder of this chapter will examine these three elements: getting to know students, building a community, and designing the physical environment of the classroom.

Getting to Know Students

An early and persistent quest for knowledge about students has at least four benefits.

1. It sends a message to each student that the teacher sees him or her as an individual, and it also suggests that he or she is interesting enough for an adult to want to know better. In this way, students begin to trust the teacher—to believe that the teacher will be an advocate and support system in the classroom—and shed the anonymity and alienation they might feel in the classroom.

2. It contributes to a student's willingness to do the difficult work of learning. Students work for people they value (i.e., people who value them).

3. It helps the teacher accept responsibility for the student's success. We invest most deeply in the people we really know—those with whom we have a relationship and those who are "three dimensional" to us. It's difficult to let those individuals down.

4. It provides an open and continually expanding window into each student as an individual and a learner. Understanding a student's culture, likes and dislikes, personal sense of possibility as a learner, relationships with peers, home support, dreams, strengths and vulnerabilities, and preferred ways of learning make it possible for a teacher to plan approaches to curriculum and instruction that have a higher likelihood of facilitating success for individual learners and for the class as a whole.

Teachers use an incredibly wide array of strategies to get to know their students as the year begins and to continue to learn about them as the year progresses. Consider the following examples:

- An elementary teacher had her students play a "getting to know you" game in which her 4th graders searched for classmates who had particular attributes (See Figure 4.1). After the game, the teacher asked students to look at patterns in their classroom. She said, "Everyone who has an unusual pet, please come stand by me at the front of the room and tell us about your pet." She then said, "If you said you like helping out at school or home, raise your hand." To those students, she said, "Tomorrow, we'll begin to assign some important jobs in our classroom. I hope you'll consider signing up for one of those roles."

  During the game and ensuing activity, the teacher took notes on student data sheets and later alphabetized and accompanied her notes with photos she took of her students on the first day of school. She systematically added to the notes throughout the year as she observed students, talked with them, and generated preassessment and formative assessment information. She sometimes used the sheets in conversations with students, and she sometimes used them in parent conferences—showing parents what she was learning and inviting them to contribute their own insights. She often used them to plan lessons that were designed in response to her students' varied interests and needs. By the end of the school year, each student was represented by multiple data sheets and a "learner biography."

Figure 4.1
"Getting to Know You" Game

Name: _____

See if you can find at least one classmate who matches each category. When you find someone, write his or her name in the box for that category. See how many matches you can find before time is up.

I have three or more brothers and sisters.	I have been to more than two schools since 1st grade.	I can say a poem from memory.	I have a very unusual pet.	I have read at least one *Harry Potter* book.
I was born far away from here.	My birthday is on a holiday.	I am a good swimmer.	I like helping out at home and at school.	I can play a musical instrument.
I can make a basket from the free-throw line.	I have ridden a horse.	I enjoy drawing and painting.	I like to use a computer.	I can speak a language other than English.
I can whistle a song.	Someone in my family is a twin.	I can count backwards from 100 really fast.	I have won an award.	I am good at Double Dutch.

- A middle school science teacher in an urban area visited the homes of each of his students during the summer and early fall of the school year. If someone was home, he introduced himself, asked to say hello to his student, and explained that he was preparing to help students understand the ecology of their neighborhoods. He told parents that he was excited about getting to know their children and asked them to tell him a few things about the student that they thought were important for him to know. If no one was home, he left a printed note with much of the same information and told the parents that he wanted to personally invite them to visit him at school.

Mentally placing his students in a context helped him understand some important things about them, even before they were in his classroom. Taking the time to visit their homes sent a clear message to parents and students that he wanted to know his students. It also indicated his understanding of the value of family in the lives of his students and in their learning. He continued to call and visit parents—most often with good news, but occasionally to talk with them about specific learning needs—throughout the year.

- A high school science teacher invited her students to use the classroom during a shared lunch period as a place to study, ask questions about their work, or just eat lunches they brought from home. The room almost always had 15–20 students in it during this period, which provided the teacher with an opportunity to see her students in a more relaxed atmosphere, to observe them with one another, and to provide assistance for them with reading, labs, and projects.

One of the teacher's colleagues—a high school English teacher—favored two other strategies for learning and understanding more about her students. She held monthly book club discussions at her home and encouraged students to come and share their ideas. Sometimes students discussed issues related to class assignments, but other times they reflected topics of special interest to students or the teacher. The teacher always made a point of issuing special, private invitations to students she felt might be reluctant to come, and she always made sure they had safe, reliable transportation. The teacher also went to an extracurricular event every other week to see students in voluntary settings. She tried to select events that would enable her to see the broadest possible swath of her students, but when two or more groups met simultaneously, she nearly always chose to attend the event in which her less academically engaged students participated.

Figure 4.2 presents some additional ways of getting to know students, and the Teacher's Toolkit in the back of this book provides additional examples. The purpose of each of these strategies is to help teachers teach better through a deeper understanding of the individuals they teach. Teachers who are intent on knowing their students well use a variety of strategies throughout the year in service of that goal.

Central to the process of getting to know students in a differentiated classroom is the use of continual assessment. It is a good idea to keep in mind several important points, including the following:

• Early in the year, develop ways to informally check students' understanding of essential skills and knowledge in your grade/subject, such as aural comprehension, visual comprehension, reading ability, writing fluency, spelling, oral communication, and key academic vocabulary. These measures do not need not be exhaustive or time consuming; for example, you might generally assess spelling and writing fluency in a student's written response to an aural comprehension passage, or you might assess oral fluency as a student shares in a morning class meeting (younger students) or summarizes what he or she

Figure 4.2

Strategies for Getting to Know Students

Strategy	Explanation
Greetings at the Door	In all grades and subjects, teachers can learn a great deal about students and greatly enhance communication by being at the door each day to speak briefly with each student as he or she enters the room. It is difficult to overstate the significance of asking specific questions (*How did the homework go last night?*), making personal comments (*You have new shoes on today.*), and paying compliments (*I know the work was hard yesterday, so I appreciate that you stuck with it despite the difficulty.*). The accumulation of information and interpersonal connections that result are immeasurable.
"All About Me" Bags	Students bring to school five objects that help the teacher and their classmates know them better. For very young students, it's a good idea to send a letter home so someone there can help them choose the objects and assemble the bag. Students can decorate their bags to show more about themselves if they'd like. Each day, the teacher asks three or four students to share their bags and the objects inside. Continue until everyone has an opportunity to share.
Communication Journals	These are journals in which students write to teachers in a conversational way. There should be a secure place on the teacher's desk for students to place their journals when they write an entry they want the teacher to read. Students often write about what they do over the weekend, music they like, or suggestions they have for class. Occasionally, a student will write about a serious problem he or she wants the teacher to know. The teacher writes entries in response and then returns the journals. Communication journals provide the human-to-human exchanges that are sadly lacking in class.
Note Taking	There is much to be learned from careful and systematic observation of students as they work in class. It is therefore useful for a teacher to carry a checklist of required skills, for example, and to spot check each student's work for evidence of those skills. It's also helpful to jot down general observations about individual students (along with the date) which can then be "filed" and arranged by subject area or class period. These observations form a growing archive of information on each student's learning development and needs.
Surveys	It's simple to develop surveys that ask students to share their sense of themselves as learners in a particular subject, their interests, and their methods for learning effectively. These surveys can be administered at the beginning of the year to "jump start" teacher knowledge and as the year progresses to help teachers follow their students' development.
One to Ten	On a bulletin board, create a number line and label it 1 to 10. For younger students, draw an unhappy face over the 1 and a happy face over the 10. Title the board *How do you feel about ___?* The topic can change often; for example, one day students might be asked how they feel about a book they read yesterday in class, and another day they might be asked how they feel about starting a new math unit. Students then place paper dolls or name tags beneath the appropriate number to represent their feelings about that day's topic. This activity quickly illustrates the variety of feelings in the class on a particular topic, and it can also help determine the next steps in instruction. Over time, patterns will develop in individual students' responses.

recalls from yesterday's class (older students). Your sense of the student's proficiencies will progress over time, but it is nonetheless important to have a sense of where each student begins the year in terms of expected competencies—and to intervene as necessary to promote growth from the outset. Be alert to the likelihood that some students will only appear to lack knowledge, skills, or understanding when the real problem is actually a barrier to revealing what they know. Some of these barriers include poor language proficiency and difficulty with test taking and timed settings.

• Do not be overly swayed by a student's record from previous school years, by comments from other teachers about the student, or by standardized test data. The reason for this caution is to ensure that each student starts the year in your mind with all the possibilities necessary to move ahead and succeed. When a student becomes "that kid" who causes teachers to roll their eyes, who has "failed" the standardized test three years in a row, or who does poorly in science, it's difficult for a new teacher to have a growth mind-set about that student. It's also difficult for that student *not* to be aware of doubts the teacher has about his or her prospects. Likewise, if you latch on to an image of a student as the one who is always on the honor roll or who is always at the top of the class on achievement tests, your mind-set is likely to be "fixed" in regard to that student, and you will be less likely to challenge the student to see how far he or she can grow.

• Make sure students recognize that when you learn useful things about their interests, preferred ways of learning, and academic strengths and needs, you then use that information as you plan for the class. When you have insights about a student's work, be sure to share it with the student in a way that helps that individual work smarter and learn better. The goal is not for the teacher to become a "keeper of knowledge" about students, but to reflect that knowledge to students in ways and at times that give them more dominion over their own success. Consistently identify and celebrate what students can do rather than dwell on their difficulties. Building on student strengths is a direct route to student motivation, buy-in, engagement, and achievement.

• Expect students to grow and change. Resist the inclination to assume that a student who is interested in insects in September will still be passionate about that topic in March. Some will; some will not. Resist also the inclination to categorize a student according to learning preference. Most people learn differently in different subjects, when content is new versus when it is familiar, and even at different times of day. Use the information you gain through observation to provide students with options, not to lock them in to a predetermined assignment. Check back with them often to see how they change and develop.

• Remember that students are your best source of information. Let them know you want to hear when things are going well—and when they aren't. Occasionally, use exit cards, checklists, computer surveys, end-of-unit evaluations, or other simple mechanisms to invite students to share their sense of how they're doing. Be sure to use what you learn. Remember that students from some cultural groups may be more reticent to "advise" you for fear that doing so would be disrespectful. In those cases, don't push, but remind students that when they share ideas about how the class works best for everyone, it is helpful to you, and you appreciate their input.

A fundamental tenet of differentiation is that excellent teachers don't see themselves simply as teachers of content. Yes, they are fully committed to teaching content to young people, but they are also dedicated students in their own right—of the content and of their students. They believe that teaching isn't complete until learning occurs and that learning is predicated on a teacher's thorough understanding of both content and his or her students.

Building a Community in the Classroom

A community is an outgrowth of people coming together around an opportunity to discover, recognize, appreciate, and reach toward some shared world (Greene, 2000). In differentiated classrooms, a teacher leads students to craft a common vision of a class in which there is room for everyone and individuals make a commitment to support one another in learning.

Being part of a community meets a fundamental human need for acceptance, belonging, affinity, respect, and caring. It reassures us that we can be part of something bigger than ourselves. For students from cultures with a collectivistic orientation, being part of a community is fundamental to how the world operates, and feeling a strong sense of "family" in the classroom provides normalcy and security (Rothstein-Fisch & Trumbull, 2008).

Of course, not all communities are positive. Gangs and cults are examples of negative communities, but they still illustrate the basic need to be part of an identifiable circle of like-minded people who share a mission and provide one another with both an identity and a support system.

Teachers who lead students to craft a mutual vision of a differentiated classroom envision something like the democratic classroom described by James Beane (2005). In such places, student differences are not problems to be overcome, students are not separated according to their differences, and uniformity is not mandatory. Teachers in these classrooms, then, send the signal that diversity is a strength that leads to a genuinely democratic community in which young people learn to live and work together.

Beane reminds us that at the core of democracy are the related principles that people (1) have a fundamental right to human dignity; (2) have a responsibility to care about the common good, dignity, and welfare of others; (3) can see their own personal fate tied to the good of the group as a whole; and (4) have the intellectual and social capacity to work together to resolve issues as they arise. This is a high-minded vision—and the one on which the United States has based its aspirations as a nation. Enacting it is not easy, but it is important. In the classroom, as in the nation, this vision challenges and inspires us to continual self-improvement.

For students, these aspirations generally speak to a teacher's high expectations. Grappling with these goals prepares students for the world outside their classroom and requires them to take responsibility for their thoughts, actions, and reactions—both in their own work and as part of a team. Thus, being part of a sound community in a differentiated classroom addresses a fundamental human need for affinity with a group, which, in turn, leads to the higher goals of self-realization and contribution to a common good.

For the teacher, leading to develop a strong classroom community adds depth to teaching. It also increases learner motivation, self-awareness, and acceptance of responsibility. Ultimately, it provides a support system that helps the teacher oversee and maintain the effective operation of a classroom designed to operate flexibly and maximize the growth of each student.

Developing community

Leading students to form a positive sense of community, of course, is tightly linked to getting to know students. As a teacher shows interest in knowing individual students and treats them with respect, others notice. It becomes evident that, in that teacher's classroom, people matter, and there are opportunities for all students to learn about one another. The class is also engaged in a conversation about creating an environment in which each person is seen as valuable and in which the growth of each person is of ultimate importance. As the conversation unfolds, the teacher continues to bring students back to the original reason for creating a classroom that is responsive to each student—each student matters. Often implicit (but occasionally explicit) in this conversation is the idea that "This is who we are. This is what we do." As a result, the group becomes more defined, and students eventually develop a better understanding of one another, see their ideas enacted, and work together with increased effectiveness. Ultimately, a community forms.

As is the case with getting to know students, there are many ways to contribute to the formation of a classroom community in which individuals share common interests and goals. Consider the following classroom examples:

- A high school English teacher came to the honest but difficult conclusion that by the time students reached her class, few had a burning desire to read more poems, complete more grammar exercises, or write additional formulaic essays. She understood that she would have to create a classroom in which students felt connected in a way that made her content seem important to them. She began by creating a classroom space in which students could carry on a conversation. She told students small stories from her life, and she invited them to tell their own. "I love a good story," she often said. "I'll even delay a test for five minutes if someone has a good story to tell . . . but it better be good!" In time, she began to tell stories from her life that had more meaning. By then, her students were listening to one another with positive regard, and they trusted that they could share meaningful stories from their own lives. She helped them recognize how their stories were like those of the authors they read. She also helped them believe that their stories were worth preserving in written form. Throughout the year, she purposefully and simultaneously led students to bond around storytelling and related the material she taught to the people she taught. The class was life-shaping for her students; many of them developed into devoted readers and writers.

- A primary teacher reserved a classroom wall to post 10 calendar pages— one for each month the students were in school. The pages were large and offered ample room to write. On the first day of school, she told her students that they would be writing a class history as the year went on. "When something important happens," she said, "we'll put it on our calendar with words and drawings and pictures. That way, we can all go back and read our history as a class." Each day as school was about to end, she'd ask students to say what had been most important that day. Early in the year, she'd sometimes prompt students with, "Here are three things that seem to be important today. Is there something else you can add to that list?" She made sure to include special moments in individual students' lives (that were shared that day) and whole-class items, including both positive reinforcement (e.g., Everyone worked extra hard with math today) and room for improvement (e.g., We have to figure out how to talk more quietly when we work). Students predictably followed her modeling as they made their own suggestions for the class history. Sometimes, the teacher added photos or students provided illustrations to go with their words. As the year progressed, students began to do more of the writing on the calendar. When adults came into the room, the teacher would ask volunteers to explain the calendar and several items they felt clearly showed what the class was like. (Students nearly always showed their parents the calendar when they were in the classroom.) Increasingly, the calendar became a shared story of "who we are," "what we do," and "why our work is important."

• A middle school math teacher saw that her students were sometimes frustrated by the challenging math they were studying. One day, she offered a "jeer" for the group—a cheer with a grumpy personality. She invited students to chant the jeer with her three times in succession, with each rendition louder than the one before. When they finished, she said, "Here's our new slogan: *We gripe and conquer!*" She was surprised how the moment changed the tone in the classroom. Students vented, laughed, and worked with much less tension and hesitation than in days past. A few days later, when she noticed frustration building again, she said, "Who remembers the jeer? I think we need to practice it again." On another day, she said, "Okay, time for a jeer, but I'm getting tired of that old one. Anyone have a fresh idea?" Students began to bring in "anti-math" jeers for the class, and she used them when needed. Each time, she followed the class chants with the question, "What's our class motto?" The students responded in unison, "We gripe and conquer," and they did. The jeers were one of many techniques the teacher used to bring her students together as conquerors of math, rather than victims of it. Students routinely came back to visit the teacher after they graduated, and they inevitably told her that they remembered the lesson she taught them: It's okay to get frustrated, but it's not okay to give up.

- A high school French teacher put a cupcake on a student's desk on his birthday. She stood by the student's desk as class began, wished the student a happy birthday, and acknowledged two or three things about the student that she particularly valued. The students applauded and class went on. The importance of this small gesture might be easy to overlook. However, it was evidenced by a quiet student in the class who had an opportunity to travel abroad with her parents later that year. This student was very excited about the trip because she would have a chance to speak French and bring some things back for the class. Shortly before the trip, though, she told her mother she couldn't go and asked her to get a refund for her ticket. The mother, puzzled and not very pleased, asked her daughter why she suddenly felt she couldn't go on the trip. Her daughter replied, "I didn't realize the trip was during the week of my birthday. I'd miss my cupcake in French. I have to be there for that!" It wasn't the cupcake that the student would miss, of course, it was the teacher's public acknowledgement of her value and what it communicated to the class that made the day more important than the trip. The cupcake ritual modeled an ethic of respect and appreciation that pervaded everything in the classroom. It was one of many ways the teacher led the students to conclude, "This is who we are, and this is how we treat one another in here."

Teachers develop their own strategies to identify and clarify the specific goals to which they aspire as a class. In doing so, they not only clarify what matters most in the classroom, but they help students come together around those significant ideas. They do not emphasize community in lieu of content, but rather as a means of opening students to the learning process. Figure 4.3 and the Teacher's Toolkit contain more examples of methods teachers can use to build a more positive classroom community.

Using student groups and classroom community

In differentiated classrooms, the use of student groups is integral to building a productive, positive community, but it's not the only requirement. In fact, effectively differentiated classrooms will inevitably require students to work independently or in whole-class sessions. Theoretically, at least, it might be possible to differentiate without ever having students work in small groups. Except for concerns about classroom control, however, it's difficult to understand why a teacher would want to do that.

Figure 4.3
Strategies for Building a Classroom Community

Strategy	Explanation
Purposeful Talk	Teachers in many elementary classrooms use morning meetings to provide time for students to greet one another, set a tone, plan ahead, reflect, and model behaviors. These meetings allow teachers to spotlight things that matter to individuals and to the group. They also allow students to hear and respond to one another, thus defining what matters most in the classroom and what will come to define the community.
	Teachers in middle and high school classrooms make similar use of very brief segments of time at the beginning or end of class to share anecdotes, reflect on what recently transpired in class, plan for what's ahead, and be reminded of the ideas they are working to implement in their classroom.
Keeper of the Book	Students take turns keeping notes (in a notebook or on the computer) to log what is taking place during a particular class, directions for projects, and assignment deadlines. If a student is absent or just uncertain about the reason for a task, task requirements, or criteria for success, the logbook will provide support and guidance. Students support one another's success in this way and also learn to take pride in the quality of their entries when it's their turn to be "keeper of the book."
Integrating New Students	Current students in a class make plans to welcome and integrate new students—they decide what is necessary to make sure new students feel welcomed and are ready to join the class in the work they are doing. Students accept various roles in this process, and the class debriefs throughout the year to continue to enhance their plans.
Welcoming Guests to the Classroom	Students play an active role when parents, other teachers, administrators, or community members come to their classroom. Depending on the nature of the guest and visit, students make sure guests are welcomed, have a place to sit, have copies of student assignments, observe or participate in student conversations, and receive explanations about the nature of the classroom community. Students can play different roles in the process, and roles can change over time. In a differentiated classroom, students should quickly be able to explain and illustrate the classroom philosophy and practice for guests.
Working on a Sustained and Meaningful Product	Students in elementary school can build a model of their community throughout the year, or they can establish communication or raise funds for other students of their age in a part of the world they are studying.
	Middle school students can study the developmental needs of young children while they examine award-winning children's books as a way to understand the elements of literature. Ultimately, they can write and illustrate a library of books for primary students in a feeder school, read their books to those students, and lead discussions on the books.
	High school students can develop and publish a science magazine for elementary or middle school students that relate important science concepts to the personal interests of those students.
Model What Matters	It's essential for all teachers to model classroom behaviors they want their students to exhibit. This means listening respectfully to each student's ideas and questions, demonstrating positive regard for student differences, complimenting legitimate student accomplishments, and politely but firmly rejecting behaviors that undermine the efforts of anyone in the group. Students should also see their teachers use these principles as they work with colleagues and associates in the school.

When student groups function effectively, they are highly motivating to students. They provide an opportunity for students to share ideas, get input, encounter alternative ways of approaching problems or tasks, and get support. For many students, this is a precursor to successful learning. Groups also make the classroom more efficient for teachers who can, for example, more effectively focus on five or six groups than on 30 individuals. In Chapter 6, we'll look at procedures for helping students work effectively in groups. Here, though, we'll spotlight some principles of effective grouping that support the beliefs and practices of differentiation.

Use flexible grouping. A nonnegotiable aspect of effective differentiation is that teachers plan a consistent flow of varied student groupings within a unit of study based on the nature of the work and the individual needs of students. This allows students to see themselves and one another in a variety of learning contexts, and it provides the teacher with regular opportunities to observe each student in multiple contexts. For example, Benjamin may be scheduled to work four days this week with peers who have similar readiness levels and skill needs. However, the teacher's plan for literacy groups during the week should also, for instance, include opportunities for Benjamin to share some reading with students who have similar interests regardless of their readiness needs, to work with another group of students who choose to express what they learn in a particular format, to work independently at a center, and to work with a student of his choice to discuss class material. Students perform and learn differently in different circumstances; they deserve the opportunity to work with varied peer groupings on a regular and consistent basis so they can see themselves, and are seen by others, as multidimensional learners.

Teach up. Design group tasks to ensure that each student works with a rich curriculum and has to think about and apply essential ideas and skills. Occasionally, a student or group will need time to practice a discrete skill, but there should not be student groups that consistently practice skills out of context while other group tasks cast students as thinkers, problem solvers, and creators. Begin by planning tasks that challenge advanced learners, and then scaffold as needed for learners who are less advanced. Teaching in this way is an indicator of a growth mind-set teacher, and it will be an advantage to virtually all learners.

Use multiple ability tasks. Such tasks have more than one right answer or way to solve a problem, are intrinsically interesting and rewarding to a variety of students, allow different students to make different contributions to the successful completion of a task, and require a variety of skills and strengths for successful completion (Cohen, 1994). Multiple ability tasks often draw on a variety of media because of their high relevance to students, the access they provide to important content, and the opportunities they allow for students to express learning. These tasks also emphasize the critical importance of reading and writing to student success.

Assign individual roles within groups. Individual roles ensure that each student has a genuinely important academic or intellectual contribution to make to the task. For example, if one student in a group is designated as the reader and another is the timekeeper, it's evident to students that the reader has a more "valuable" role than the timekeeper. On the other hand, if one student is expected to diagram the steps necessary to solve a math problem and another is expected to write prose directions for solving it, each student contributes equally to the task of "demonstrating what a student who has been absent this week would have to know, understand, and be able to do in order to feel competent with the kind of math problem we've been focusing on this week." Groups in which only some members have competencies that are critical to success create a sort of caste system of winners and losers rather than contribute to a developing sense of community in the classroom.

Make content accessible to everyone. In mixed-readiness groups, ensure that written content is accessible to everyone in the group. English language learners (ELLs), for example, should have a feasible method for bridging the two languages. Recall that students cannot grow academically when work is too difficult or too easy for them, and it is inappropriate and ineffective to base a task on material a student cannot read. To deal with varied reading levels in a mixed-readiness group, one student can be designated as the group's reader, text or directions can be recorded, or students can read materials at different levels of complexity and then work together on a common and related task.

Assign competence. Observe students carefully, noting the particular strengths, skills, and insights they bring to group work. When you see a worthy and honest contribution, remark on what you saw. For example, say, "I think the question Sherisa just asked was a significant one. It caused you to rethink the line of logic you were using as a group. The ability to ask a challenging question at the right time is a very useful skill." It's important for all students to receive this sort of affirmation, but it's particularly important for students who may be seen as having lower status among their peers to hear—and for their peers to hear—such comments from a teacher when they are genuinely warranted.

Effective use of instructional group work benefits individual students in terms of their academic development. It also contributes to a sense of classroom community as students consistently have opportunities to work with a broad range of classmates on a variety of tasks designed to ensure that everyone is a meaningful contributor to the shared assignment.

Designing a Physical Environment to Support Learning

As is the case with all other classroom elements, the goal of planning the physical environment of a classroom is to maximize opportunities for teaching and learning. To that end, the physical environment in a differentiated classroom should provide the structure and predictability young people need in order to feel secure. In addition, it should allow flexibility to attend to both group and individual needs in the context of a rich, meaning-focused curriculum.

In very much the same way that a person is represented by his or her clothing and personal hygiene, a classroom's environment also communicates a good bit about what that classroom is like. It speaks subtly, or not so subtly, about the nature and philosophy of the teacher, the degree of organization that's likely to characterize the classroom, and the teacher's concern for students and their success.

We'll briefly examine three elements that teachers should consider carefully as they arrange the classroom. Decisions regarding each of them contribute to or detract from a focus on learning. A classroom does not have to be "upscale" to be thoughtful, organized, and flexible; nor does it have to be "upscale" to communicate the seriousness with which the teacher considers the success of each learner.

As we have suggested, a differentiated classroom is student focused. It therefore carries the expectation that students will

- Increase their proficiency and comfort while working independently, in small groups, and as a whole class.
- Think at high levels—they will comprehend and apply what they learn.
- Support the learning of their peers actively and effectively.
- Help the teacher make the classroom work.

Further, a differentiated classroom carries the expectation that the teacher will

- Study students consistently in order to teach them more effectively.
- Build a community in the classroom intentionally and explicitly.
- Work with individuals, small groups, and the whole class on a regular basis.
- Use flexible student groupings.
- Address the readiness, interest, and learning profile needs of each individual learner.

Furniture arrangement and floor plan

We can make some decisions about a classroom's furniture arrangement and floor plan that directly support the above student and teacher expectations. Two useful questions that teachers should ask when they think about furniture arrangement and floor plan are (1) What are all of my options? and (2) Which of my options best align with the goals I have for myself and my students? Here are some guidelines to consider as you think about your classroom's furniture and floor plan.

- When possible, opt to use tables—or tables and individual desks—instead of individual desks only. Straight rows of desks do little to invite or facilitate meaningful collaboration. If new furniture is not an option, many schools and districts have storage areas full of furniture that is no longer used. Discarded tables can be covered easily with poster board or heavy construction paper to make the best-looking furniture in the school.

- Consider arranging four to eight individual seats or desks in one area of the room. Despite the general desirability of tables over individual desks, this sort of "independent study" area can be useful for students who need to work alone on a particular assignment, who are having a bad day, who have been absent and need to make up work, or who struggle with emotions and need to have some time away from peers.

- Arrange the room so that you can easily walk among students. This is essential for students to feel your presence and for you to observe students while they work. It also allows you to reach each student easily when they require assistance.

- Arrange student seating areas (including carpet seating for young learners) in a way that accounts for individuals' responses to "private space" as much as possible. When students are seated too close to one another, some begin to feel threatened. Others simply take advantage of the opportunity to "reach out and touch someone," which can create unnecessary problems. On the other hand, some students benefit from physical proximity to peers as they work. As with most other elements, planning for flexibility to address a variety of needs is essential.

- Position your desk in an out-of-the-way place, instead of front and center. The latter option takes up much valuable real estate and puts the emphasis in the wrong place. In an effectively differentiated classroom, a teacher's desk will be used very little!

• Plan multiple furniture arrangements that support varied tasks and are beneficial for whole-class discussions, small-group work (pairs, triads, and quads), and individual work.

• Plan one arrangement that encourages student-to-student discussion. This would likely be in the shape of a *U*, a circle, or two semicircles that face each other. Straight and orderly rows of desks that face the teacher are better suited to an adult talking at students rather than students talking and listening to one another. With younger students, this need is often met with a designated space where everyone sits on a rug to listen to directions or share ideas.

• Try to line a significant portion of the room with shelving, cabinets, cubbyholes, mailboxes, or other structures that allow you to house a variety of materials, supplies, and artifacts. Look for discarded shelves if necessary, and get students to help paint them. Shelves made from bricks, cinder blocks, and board planks also work just fine!

• Think about the location of "specialty" areas, such as science lab space, listening stations, computer centers, and learning/interest centers. If these areas will be set up most (or all) of the time, and if students will need to use them independently or in small groups, they should be clearly visible to you at all times but out of sight for students who will not use them.

Wall space and bulletin boards

These environmental elements serve a dual purpose. They can humanize a classroom, and they can also contribute considerably to learner independence and success. The stereotypical classroom image tends to be of blank walls and bulletin boards filled with cutout images from teacher stores—which, of course, do little to facilitate student success or make the class seem more learner oriented. Consider the following suggestions when you think about wall space and bulletin boards in the classroom.

• If you will use student assignment charts, be sure to reserve a large and prominent place to post them. Make certain they are large enough for students to see from anywhere in the room.

• Designate some wall or bulletin board space that will predictably contain information about key assignments—for example, criteria for success, suggested resources, due dates, and reminders.

• Consider creating a "hint board" or "hint cards" where you can collect reminders of how to do things that students need to know but may have forgotten. For example, if students learned about haiku poetry last month and will now write a haiku to express their feelings about something they are studying in science, the hint board/cards might contain the elements of haiku in addition to a few illustrations. Hint boards and cards help students work more independently and thus preserve teacher time to work with individuals and small groups. Figure 4.4 illustrates examples of material that might be included on hint cards.

Figure 4.4
Examples of Hint Cards

Hint: How to solve for X

1. Look at the question. Is it an equation? If yes...
2. Put all x's on one side of the equal sign and all numbers on the other.
3. Solve for x by doing simple arithmetic. Remember that X is also a number, so you have to do math on that side of the equation, too.
4. Finish all arithmetic steps until only one X remains.
5. Check to see if this value for X works in your original equation.

Example:
$$3x - 2 = 4 + x$$
$$3x - x = 4 + 2$$
$$2x = 6$$
$$x = \frac{6}{2} = 3$$
$$3(3) - 2 = 4 + (3)$$
$$9 - 2 = 7 \checkmark$$

Hint: How to read maps

1. Look at the legend box on your map. Are you looking at the right country? Its name should be on top.
2. Read the symbols on the legend to learn about your country...
... Look at the symbols and find them on your map. The star will tell you the capital, blue will tell you where the water is, green will tell you where the land is.
3. Every legend has a scale. This will help you with tasks such as knowing the distance from city to city and the size of your country.

name
Mexico
— border
★ capital
···· river
⋀ mountain
ⵜ scale

- Designate space that will contain a few exemplars of high-quality student work from past years for ongoing assignments. In a differentiated classroom, there may need to be exemplars at varied levels of complexity for a single assignment—differentiated by readiness or by different modes of expression (when students have an option to express their work in varied ways). All exemplars, however, should meet the criteria for success. This area should also contain rubrics or other means of helping students see *why* posted exemplars are, in fact, exemplary.

- Designate space that will feature attractively posted, frequently changing examples of high-quality student work (both individual and group work) that has recently been completed.

- Designate some wall space that can intentionally remain blank. Use this area to create a working space for students who may be distracted by visual stimulation and who will concentrate better if they look at "plain" walls.

- Try to find wall space, bulletin board space, or shelf space where you and your students can place objects or materials that are personally interesting, or where students and student achievements can be featured. Figure 4.5 provides one teacher-developed example of a space that features students throughout the year. The middle school teacher who developed this idea uses one bulletin board to spotlight five students each week. She teaches approximately 150 students, and, every month, she asks approximately 20 students to complete a "Here's Somebody Who" template along with a few relevant photos. (Preparing the board takes very little time since students do most of the work.) She asks students to mount their templates and photos on bright cardboard, and when it is time to change the displays, she returns the previous ones and encourages students to give their displays to a parent, grandparent, or someone else important to them. She adds, "Please tell them that I'm grateful for the opportunity to teach you." The board has been very popular with all of her students, and most students enjoy reading about their peers who are featured.

Materials, supplies, and organizers

Just as the appropriate use of furniture, floor space, and wall space is critical to facilitate learner success and support flexibility in the classroom, careful planning for placement of materials, supplies, and organizing elements can also help achieve these goals. The idea is to give students access to what they will need as they work in

Figure 4.5
"Here's Somebody Who" Bulletin Board

Here's somebody who . . .

Likes _____

Really likes _____

Really, really likes _____

Doesn't like _____

Really doesn't like _____

Really, really doesn't like _____

Has changed from _____ to _____

Is proud of _____

Wishes people knew _____

Is willing to work hard for _____

Dreams about _____

Will someday be _____

Is already _____

Whose name is _____

a way that maximizes efficiency and minimizes disruption. By preplanning these elements with student success in mind, teachers contribute to each student's sense of both individual and group competence. Consider the following suggestions when you think about materials, supplies, and organizers in the classroom.

- Store materials and supplies that will be used often (e.g., books, paper, markers/crayons, rulers, lab supplies, headphones) in places where students can access them easily—without having to walk through work areas—and in view of the teacher. If necessary, use more "remote" areas of the room for materials or supplies that students will use less often or that fewer students will use.

- Store materials and supplies that should be unavailable to students in places where it is difficult for students to see or access—for example, high shelves or cabinets, file cabinets, or a storage area behind the teacher's desk. Be sure to designate these areas as off-limits to students. These materials might include equipment the teacher will need, supplies for upcoming units, or materials that will be used by a few students with special needs at some time during the year.

• Use bins, tubs, or boxes where possible to keep supplies organized and neat rather than having them spread out on tables or shelves.

• Designate and label places in the room where students will turn in classwork and homework as they complete it. In elementary classrooms, where teachers teach multiple subjects, it makes sense to have different boxes or trays for each subject. Use icons and/or color coding to help students know where to place their work if they are just learning how to read or if there are ELLs in the classroom.

• Have students use file folders to organize work that is "in process" (e.g., check-lists of completed work, mastered skills, books read). It's helpful to color code these folders for secondary classes where teachers have multiple classes. For example, write students' names on the folders in blue for first period, green for second period, and so on. It's also useful to have color-coded boxes or crates for each class from which folders can be retrieved and to which they can be returned.

• Designate a place in the room where students will go to find anchor activities.

• Have more than one pencil sharpener and trash can in the classroom, and make sure they are in locations that are easily accessed with minimal distraction for other students, or provide sharpened pencils in a cup or box so students don't need to use the pencil sharpener.

Decisions about the use of furniture, floor space, wall areas, bulletin boards, materials, supplies, and classroom organizers will vary somewhat among grades, subjects, and schools, and with the confidence of the teacher. It is *not* the case, however, that these issues are relevant only to the lower grades. From preschool through high school, the most effective teachers make judicious use of every resource at their disposal to maximize their own—and their students'—efficiency and effectiveness. In Chapters 5 and 6, we'll look at ways in which classroom routines allow flexibility and extend academic growth. Chapter 5 will examine routines that prepare students to work in a differentiated classroom, and Chapter 6 will examine routines that are important once students begin to work in a differentiated classroom.

5

Classroom Routines
Preparing for the Work Ahead

As with all other human characteristics, learning is diverse and different for each learner. It is a function of heredity, experience, perspectives, backgrounds, talents, interests, capacities, needs, and the unpredictable flow of any particular life. . . . It is exactly this diversity that provides innumerable opportunities for expanding learning—first, by acknowledging differences in physiological, personal, linguistic, cultural, and social backgrounds, and second by focusing on the common features that make all of us human. But the differences must be taken into account as well to provide all learners with the necessary opportunities for learning and self-development.

—Lorna Earl, *Assessment as Learning*

Classroom Procedures and Routines

Classroom procedures and routines are prescribed ways of doing things that allow teaching and learning to proceed in a structured, predictable, and efficient manner. Their purpose should be clear to both teacher and students—

they exist to help students learn as effectively as possible. They should be methods to build student competence, not mechanisms to control students. Regardless of the procedure or routine, there are important steps that teachers must follow.

Determine them. What routines need to be established in the classroom for things to run smoothly and for everyone to learn and grow? The number of routines will vary with students' age, the nature of the class, and the your comfort level as a leader of students. Don't try to prescribe a routine for everything students do. Micromanaging is tedious for everyone and quickly sends the message that you don't trust students and are trying to manage them rather than help them manage the details of learning. On the other hand, there should be clear routines for processes that are fundamental to the operation of the class and essential for student success, such as starting class, getting and replacing materials and supplies, and monitoring classroom noise level.

Clarify the rationale for them. Be sure to help students understand both the general rationale for a routine (e.g., so the classroom can work for everyone, so everyone can succeed as a learner) and the specific rationale for a particular routine (e.g., a neat, orderly, and organized classroom helps all students easily find the things they need to get their work done, and I spend less time cleaning and more time helping students).

Develop them. Sometimes, it makes good sense for a teacher to say, "Here's how we need to do this . . ." This is certainly true with very young students, with students who lack structure in their lives, and when there is really only one acceptable way to proceed (e.g., when working with potentially hazardous lab materials in a science class). On the other hand, when students can reasonably help a teacher develop a procedure, it builds student ownership of the ideas, student investment in making the procedures work, and student–teacher partnerships in making the entire classroom work. In either case, be sure the individual steps in the procedure are clearly delineated and clear to everyone. In some instances, this may mean posting the procedure for a time or giving it to students in a handout.

Teach them. Teachers know the importance of methodically teaching content, but we sometimes assume we can just tell students a procedure and they'll get it. Whatever we want students to learn, we need to teach (unless we have evidence that they already know it). Teaching a routine may mean that students literally practice the routine. For younger students, it might mean that you need to model the routine so they can see what it looks like when done correctly. It might mean students review the steps aloud and from memory. Whatever it takes for students to know, understand, and be able to carry out the routine smoothly is what you need to do. Teach routines as carefully and explicitly as you would teach a mathematical operation, a comprehension strategy, or the steps to write a five-paragraph essay.

Apply them. Have students begin using the routine in their work. Ask them to recall the reason(s) for the routine, its steps, and how it should look and sound as it is implemented.

Automatize them. In truth, a routine is a procedure that has become automatic—in other words, it's a procedure that is routine! To help students automatize a routine, use that routine multiple times in a relatively short period of time.

Reflect on, revise, and review them. It's always important to observe students as they use a routine, take notes about on the process, and reflect on the degree to which the routine is contributing to effective and efficient teaching and learning. Again, it sometimes makes sense to say, "Yesterday, I noticed that several students were having difficulty getting the help they needed while I was working with a small group. Today, I'm going to have two 'experts of the day' available instead of just one. Let's see if that makes things smoother for you." On the other hand, it can be very powerful for a teacher to work with students and reflect on how well a procedure worked. They can then engage the students to revise the procedures as needed. Students often understand a problem before the teacher, and they nearly always have insightful suggestions about how to make things operate more smoothly. It's important to review routines from time to time to maintain clarity of understanding and consistency in application. This can be particularly useful after vacations or when students have not used a particular routine for a while.

Teachers will vary in the pace at which they introduce and implement classroom routines. It makes sense to let the routines evolve in a way that feels comfortable to both teacher and students. Some teachers will introduce most or all of their standard routines during the first week of school, and their students will follow the routines comfortably and proficiently within a few days. Others will practice one routine for several days before introducing another. The unique nature of both the teacher and students will set the pace. In general, however, it is a good idea to invest time in teaching and implementing routines as early in the year as possible. This prevents students from learning one way of "doing business" early in the year only to unlearn it as the year continues. Successfully enacting the routines fundamental to a classroom is necessary in order to create the orderly, flexible classroom that supports both complex thinking and differentiation. Students will benefit from working in this sort of environment as soon as it's feasible for them to do so.

Classroom Rules to Live By

Working with students at the beginning of the year to establish classroom rules, guidelines, and agreements is useful for several reasons. First, developing the rules can either lead to or reinforce the fundamental tenets of differentiation. Second, when a teacher asks his or her class to reach a consensus about the rules by which the group will live, it sends a distinct message that the teacher trusts the students to have good judgment. Third, as students discuss and listen to one another's ideas, a general tone and specific procedures begin to emerge for what it means to think and solve problems as a group. The evolution of community begins.

Some educators, however, make a reasonable argument for *not* establishing classroom rules. Generally, their sense is that a list of rules is unnecessary when curriculum, instruction, and learning environment work as they should—and that when they don't work as they should, a list of rules can't fix what's wrong. While there's truth in this perspective, it's also the case that crafting a set of guidelines for living and working well together is fundamental to a democracy and establishes a baseline for everything that will follow. Our persuasion is that a brief set of guidelines, operating principles, or rules can provide a sense of direction for the class and a touchstone for later discussions about the nature of the class and its goals. Such a set of guidelines can also provide the rationale for basic classroom procedures and routines. They should also, in our opinion, point to an intrinsic and positive (rather than extrinsic and punitive) way of operating in the classroom.

The following examples of classroom rules have several things in common. They are brief. They are positive in tone. They challenge students. They transfer into the world beyond the classroom door.

- Be nice.
- Work hard.
- No shortcuts.
- No excuses.

A middle school teacher asks her students to think about, add to, or revise two contracts with themselves:

- I will be the student I need to be in order to become the person I ought to be.
- I will practice the Platinum Rule. (The Golden Rule asks that we treat others the way we'd like to be treated. The Platinum Rule asks that we treat others the way they'd like to be treated.)

A 4th grade class crafts a set of rules to live by. The teacher writes them on a poster and makes them available for several days so students can review them. Ultimately, each student who agrees to abide by the rules signs the poster—along with the teacher—and it is hung in the classroom so everyone can see it and refer to it for the remainder of the year.

- We agree to give *respect* to people, feelings, space, property, and ideas.
- We agree to be *responsible* for our actions, words, and choices
- We agree to show *appreciation* for others and be inclusive and friendly.
- We agree to be *X-factor learners* and positive role models—modeling excellence, can-do attitudes, and our personal best!

A high school teacher uses three rules with her students. They are terse and point to a way of life in the classroom that is enriching and empowering for all students.

- Take care of yourself.
- Take care of each other.
- Take care of this place.

Carrie Rothstein-Fisch and Elise Trumbull (2008) suggest the following straightforward and powerful rules:

- I am the best I can be.
- I follow directions the first time I hear them.
- I respect others as I wish to be respected.
- Be serious about learning.
- Be respectful.

Rather than sounding distrustful of students or overburdening them with long lists of dos and don'ts, these sets of guidelines all set a tone of high expectations. They establish what's necessary and move learning to the foreground. Sometimes, of course, students will test or violate the rules. Even adults sometimes find it difficult to adhere to principles that ask much of them. Certainly, young people sometimes find it challenging to do what they know they should do. In Chapter 7, we'll propose some ideas for responding to students who push back and challenge classroom rules.

The remainder of this chapter, though, will suggest procedures and routines that are common in differentiated classrooms and prepare students for working in such an environment. To help students learn and enact these routines, teachers should be sure to lead students to frequently consider the importance of the routines in creating a classroom that is effective for everyone, the role that classroom rules play, and how to make the routines function as they should.

Starting the Day, Starting Class

Students in the elementary grades typically enter a classroom in the morning and remain there for much of the day. As students progress through the grades, they tend to move from class to class. Although these two patterns present different opportunities and challenges for teachers, an effective beginning to the day (or to the class period) will likely address two needs regardless of age or grade. First, the beginning of the day or class should establish an affective tone that supports teaching and learning. Second, it should focus the students on learning. Whether they enter a new elementary or secondary classroom, students will be switching environments and need to focus their attention on the expectations inherent to the new environment. To help students begin the day or class in a way that supports learning, think about incorporating the following steps into your start-up routine.

Use assigned or "home base" seats. When students have a specific place to sit as class begins, it's far more efficient for the teacher to take attendance, have materials and supplies positioned efficiently, and return student work. Most elementary students do have assigned or home base seats, at least in part because they store their own materials where they sit. There is a greater debate among middle and high school teachers about whether to assign seats, with some feeling that older students should have the privilege of choosing where to sit or that it's more respectful of students to let them make that choice. Our sense is that in a differentiated classroom, students will move often and need to understand that. Assigning seats is not a control mechanism, but it is rather a way to begin the day or class efficiently and with predictability. This same efficiency and predictability also come into play at the end of the day or class when students return to their seats. This makes it easier to be sure materials and supplies are returned to appropriate places and that desks are clean and clear. It also facilitates common closure to class when students have been working on differentiated assignments. In addition, using assigned seats as class begins and ends, and on days when whole-class instruction is central, allows the teacher to avoid some common classroom seating "hazards" such as students opting out of participation by sitting in the back of the room, students arranging themselves by ethnic group, the "haves" in one part of the room and the "have nots" in another, and cliques or "clots" of best buddies sitting together and lacking the maturity to focus on learning when compelling distractions are nearby.

Be sure students know start-up expectations. Is there a particular place students should put their backpacks? Is there a board in the classroom they should check as they enter to get directions for picking up materials, beginning a task, or reviewing yesterday's work? Is there a place students should turn in homework as they enter the room, or someone who will check in their homework? Will there be a "sponge task" that students should begin as they get seated? If so, how long will they have to do the task? What purpose will it serve (e.g., review, thinking ahead, warming up)? Should they turn it in or keep the work when they finish? If you formally begin class before they finish the task, will you draw on what they have done as you begin conversation with the class? Must students be in their seats before a tardy bell begins to ring or before announcements begin? Should their desks be cleared or should books or notebooks be on their desks and ready for the start of class? What will signal the formal start of class—the teacher's voice, a bell, announcements? How should students respond to this signal? When students are clear about all of these sorts of expectations, the importance of the work of the class is highlighted. Order and predictability also contribute to a sense of safety for many students.

Use a "checking in" routine. For young students, morning meeting is a time when they can share things that are important to them and reconnect with the group. For older learners, you should take a bit of time to share a story, compliment the class or individual students on an achievement, or elicit some input about the way the class is working—and you should invite students to do the same. Effective teaching and learning are as much social and human endeavors as they are cognitive processes. Investing time in building a growing web of human connections will yield significant dividends in terms of trust, understanding, appreciation, community, and motivation to learn.

Review work plans. Be sure students know what they need to do, what high-quality work will look like, when and how to help one another (and when not to do so), how to access materials and supplies, and what to do when they finish a task. After students are comfortable with classroom routines, only a quick review or reminder will be necessary, but it's better to orient students for success than to handle the inevitable glitches that arise if students aren't clear about expectations.

Ending the Day, Ending Class

Just like the beginning of the day or class, it's important to end with clarity, purpose, and connections as well. Predictable routines for closure continue to provide parameters for an orderly, flexible classroom. They are also a key component in developing a sense of community in a differentiated classroom. Think about the following ideas as you develop your own routines for ending the day or class.

Give students advance notice. If students are working in small groups, give them a three- to five-minute signal to conclude their work and return materials and supplies to the appropriate places. Consider assigning only one or two students in each group to return materials and supplies and turn in the group's work. These roles should be assigned by you or determined by the group before work begins. Make sure students understand the need to keep the space in which they have been working clean, clear, and organized so everything is ready for the next day or class.

Signal a return to "home base." Give students a one-minute signal when you want them to begin moving back to their assigned seats. This may be achieved most efficiently by moving quietly among the groups to give them a verbal signal. It can also be done with a quick flick of the light switch or with an electronic timer on a whiteboard. Students should understand that they are expected to be in their seats by the end of the minute. Make sure students also know whether they will need supplies ready or a clear desk upon their return to "home base."

Remember to save time for closure. It's important to leave enough time at the end of the day or class to give a quick formative assessment, review how procedures and routines worked, look ahead to tomorrow, or review homework assignments. Most classes or days should end with two elements that are particularly important. First, there should be a brief closure discussion in which you review and/or students share common learning for the day or class. This not only solidifies for students the intended outcomes of their work, but it also reminds them of the important reality that, even though students in a differentiated classroom may sometimes work in different ways, they all work toward common goals and shared understandings. Second, there should once again be time to recognize the humanity of those who share the classroom. You might simply say, "When I go home today, I'm looking forward to playing with my new puppy—once I clean up after him! What are some of you looking forward to?" Alternatively, you might say, "I felt good that each of you was able to make a dent in the assignments you were doing today. I think two things contributed to that. The first is that you're getting really good at listening to directions in a way that helps you get right into your work. The second is that you've gotten quite skilled at helping one another get unstuck when you have a problem. Tell me how you're feeling about those things." It doesn't take long to renew each student's awareness of his or her interest in and commitment to the individuals in the class and the group as a whole.

Be sure students recognize their dismissal signal. This signal should nearly always come from you, not a bell or announcement. You should make every effort to be ready to dismiss students as soon as the bell sounds or the announcements are complete, but in the few instances where it's useful for students to stay in place for a moment or two longer in order for the class to end smoothly, the teacher needs to mark the end of the day or class.

Assigning Students to Groups

Teachers need to address two questions when they assign students to flexible groupings in a differentiated classroom. First, how will students know who they are working with on a particular day and at a particular time? Second, how will groups and individuals know where to work in the classroom? The ideas below provide guidance as you think about procedures to indicate and clarify answers to these questions for students.

Create "standing groups." These groups might last for a week, a month, or a unit. This develops familiar groups that will repeat, thus reducing the need to rethink student groupings every day or two. However, it's important to note that standing groups should not be permanent or even semi-permanent readiness groups. Rather, they should augment readiness-based groups, which should change often based on preassessment and formative assessment data. In addition to fluid readiness groups, other more temporary groupings should also be used along with standing groups. For example, you may ask students to turn to their neighbors to summarize an idea, to count off by sixes and then form groups of students with the same numbers, or to work in groups to demonstrate what they understand about the science concept in a diagram, a prose explanation, a model, or a set of storyboards. Figure 5.1 illustrates the way some teachers think about standing groups in elementary classrooms. Note that the name of the group does not indicate the time of day it will meet. A "10:00 group" may meet at 2:15 on Mondays and not at all on Tuesdays. The time designation is simply the name of the group. The teacher moves the hands of a cardboard clock to signal which of the groupings students will work with at a given time. Figure 5.2 provides an example of standing groups in a middle school class.

Figure 5.1
Standing Groups in an Elementary Classroom

10:00 Groups

Similar Interest
or
Strength-Based Pairs

11:00 Groups

Mixed
Readiness
Quads

Grouping by the Clock

1:00 Groups

Similar Readiness
Triads or Quads

2:00 Groups

Student-Selected
Triads

Figure 5.2
Standing Groups in a Middle School Classroom

Text Teams	Think Tanks
reading pairs composed of students with similar reading levels	mixed-readiness writing idea generator groups of four or five
Synthesis Squads	**Dip Sticks**
groups of four with varied learning strengths (e.g., visual, performance, writing, metaphorical, analytical)	groups of six with varied learning profiles, used by the teacher to do quick "dip stick" checks for progress and understanding
Teacher Talkers	**Peer Partners**
groups of five to seven with similar learning needs and with whom the teacher will meet to extend and support growth	student-selected groups of three or four used for a variety of purposes

---

Code different areas of the room. When you develop student groups (other than standing groups), create a system to designate or code areas of the room in a sort of shorthand that lets students readily know where they should move. This process allows you to attend to both group composition and working location simultaneously. For example, a high school teacher refers to four quadrants of the room as the cardinal directions (north, south, east, and west). If the teacher says, "I'd like these students to meet in the south," everyone knows instantly what is meant. Sometimes, the teacher uses additional regions such as northwest or southeast, but once students understand the layout, they can move quickly to the correct area. Other teachers might label table areas with numbers. For example, a round table in the corner is "Area 1," a nest of tables by the window is "Area 2," and so on. Another option is to put a floor plan or seating chart on an overhead projector. Students' names are written in the places where they should work on the upcoming task. The teacher simply says, "Please find your name on the chart and move quickly and quietly to the place where you'll be working today." Some names would appear in pairs, some in triads, some in quads, and some alone. The teacher might then say, "Find your name and the names of people you'll work with today if you're going to be part of a group. When I ask you to move, those of you who will be working independently, please go to the desks in the independent study area of the room. Those who will be working in pairs, please go to the front, right corner of the room. Those working in groups of three should go to the front, left corner of the room. Groups of four will be working in the back half of the room." Regardless of how you "code" the room, the goal is to give students a quick and clear indicator of where they will move for a particular task and who, if anyone, they'll be working with.

Use pocket charts or assignment boards. Teachers of younger students often use pocket charts to let students know which tasks they'll be working on at a given time and who else may be working with them on the task (See Figure 5.3). Teachers of older students can use assignment boards for the same purpose (See Figure 5.4). In both cases, students learn early in the year that certain activities are always located in the same areas of the room—for example, they need to go to a long table by the chalkboard when it's their turn to meet with the teacher, sit on the carpet in the front of the room to work with math flash cards, or go to the independent study area when they revise their writing. Pocket charts, task boards, and similar mechanisms for designating tasks and groups allow tremendous flexibility over your control of groups and assignments. They also allow for control over the duration of both groupings and assignments, while minimizing the amount of time necessary to organize students.

Giving Directions for Multiple Tasks

In a differentiated classroom, it is often the case that students will work on varied versions of the same task or even on different tasks during the same segment of time. Once students know who their working partners will be (if any) and where they should work in the classroom, they will then need clear directions for their assignment. There are many ways to be sure students know what to do as they begin working. The purpose of giving directions is, of course, student clarity about what to do and how to do it as efficiently as possible. Keeping these goals in mind can help the teacher decide which approaches make sense and which are likely to be counterproductive. Here are some suggestions for giving directions when students will work on varied tasks, versions of the same task, or in varied grouping arrangements.

Give directions to only those students who need to hear them. It generally creates confusion and wastes time if you give oral directions to the whole class for several tasks or versions of tasks. Inevitably, students hear directions other than their own, or they pay attention to whose work seems "better" than theirs. There may be some occasions when it seems important to explain to the whole class how or why varied tasks are alike and different. This is sometimes reassuring to students. For example, you may explain that today, some students will use books as a resource and others will use the computer, but tomorrow, they'll switch and students who

Figure 5.3
Pocket Charts for Elementary School Classrooms

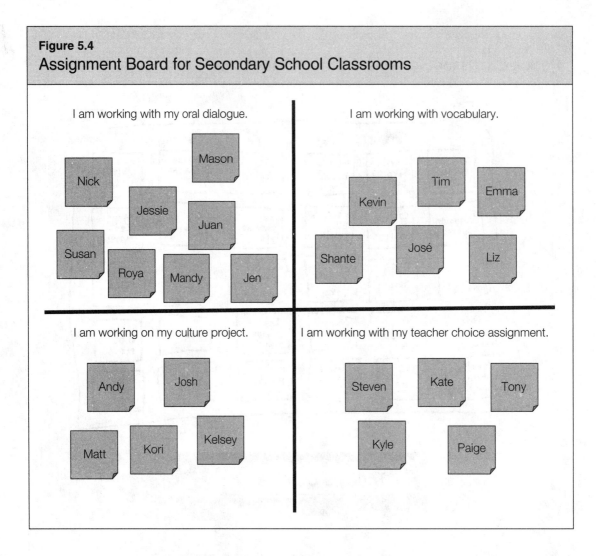

Figure 5.4
Assignment Board for Secondary School Classrooms

I am working with my oral dialogue.

I am working with vocabulary.

I am working on my culture project.

I am working with my teacher choice assignment.

used the books today will use computers tomorrow. Typically, however, it's not helpful to go over directions for tasks that certain students will not do.

Use task cards. Task cards are an effective means of giving directions to individuals or groups with varied work. In these instances, you might say, "When you move to the area of the room where you'll be working, you'll find a task card that will tell you what you need to do." Depending on the age and needs of the group, it may be wise to designate one student to read the task card to the group and then have one or two students summarize the directions before they move ahead. Task cards should clearly describe the task's goals (e.g., As a result of this work, you should be able to . . .), the steps involved, the materials needed to complete the task, and what high-quality work will look like. The latter can be addressed through class rubrics, work samples, or a statement that provides indicators of quality such as, "Your work must show that you can use fractions to solve a measurement problem. It must also show that you can accurately explain how you arrived at your solution." (See the Teacher's Toolkit for more examples.)

Provide directions in alternative formats. Recorded directions are particularly useful for young students, students who have difficulty reading, students learning English, or tasks that are multifaceted and complex. Small recorders in appropriate settings allow students to hear directions, listen to directions given in a couple of ways, or replay directions as needed while they move through their work. For students who have difficulty completing multistep tasks, recorded directions might explain each step in a task and conclude each explanation with, "Do this step now. Check it with your teacher when you finish. When she says you're ready for the next step, turn on the recording again and listen to the next part of the directions. Now turn off the recording."

Use students to give directions. In every class, there are students who are good listeners, who remember what they hear, and who explain well to others. You can give directions to such students early in a class or the day before. When it's time for the larger group to work on the assignment(s), say, "When you get to the place in the room where you'll be working, someone in your group will give you directions."

Meet with students who have difficulty understanding directions. Students can have difficulty because they are learning English, because they have attention disorders, because they find it confusing to follow multipart directions, or because they need to be close to the teacher to stay focused. Say, "I'd like to meet very briefly with the students whose names I'm going call out. You'll be joining your groups in just a minute or two." Then give directions to these students, have them paraphrase or summarize the directions, and ask them to say what steps they'll follow as they work. Students can then join their groups (or work independently) and be much more successful because of the increased clarity about what they need to do.

Differentiate the assignment. It's also possible, of course, to assign different tasks to students or ask them to pick up the correct assignment from a designated place in the room. For example, say, "The list of names on the board is in alphabetical order. Please find your name and notice the color that underlines your name. As you move to your work area for today, please pick up an assignment sheet that matches this color. For example, if your name was underlined in blue, pick up a blue assignment sheet. There are stacks of assignment sheets on the table in the front of the room and also on the bookshelves in the back of the room so we can avoid a traffic jam." Likewise, it works well to designate one student from the blue group to pick up five copies of the appropriate assignment to take to his or her group.

As students become competent and confident with these routines, they become increasingly aware of the role they play in their own learning, and they develop increasing ownership in the successful operation of the entire classroom. Chapter 6 will introduce additional routines that facilitate student and teacher success in a differentiated classroom. These routines are ones that are particularly valuable as students work in a flexible classroom setting.

6

Routines in a
Differentiated Classroom
Once the Work Begins

[We saw beginning teachers in urban settings who] had a deep understanding of how children learn and how to structure tasks so that students could successfully undertake challenging intellectual work. They knew how to develop lessons that would add up to a curriculum that could achieve central academic goals, and they knew how to use assessments that would give them diagnostic information about each child so they could target students' individual needs. They built well-functioning communities among the students and a sense of responsibility for each other's welfare.

—Linda Darling-Hammond, *The Flat World and Education*

As she discusses urban settings in which teachers often have fixed mind-sets about students; use scripted, low-level, and mechanized curricula; and aspire to run tight-ship classrooms, Linda Darling-Hammond points out that Maria, a young teacher in such an environment, and other teachers like her were able to teach a complex curriculum that typifies the work of much older students in much more affluent settings. Darling-Hammond explains how this was possible:

> Maria created an environment in which each of her students was respected and enabled to participate actively and effectively. She avoided needing to chastise students by anticipating what normal busy children are likely to do and having a plan to keep them focused, well-behaved, and engaged in learning. Her careful planning allowed students to succeed at a complex task without punishment, discouragement, conflict, or failure. (2009, p. 213)

This is the power of mindfully and proactively planning details in the classroom. Paradoxically, teachers who give meticulous care to establishing routines ultimately free their students to work. The routines spotlighted in this chapter are enacted as the work of a differentiated class takes place. They should anticipate what might go wrong in a room full of young students and prevent those problems from arising. In the end, they should make teaching and learning more effective and efficient because they support both endeavors. The routines and procedures that follow are primarily for students, but some are for teachers. For all of them, however, it's important that both students and teachers understand the goals of a differentiated classroom and how a particular routine or procedure helps achieve those goals.

Calling on Students

It's remarkably easy for teachers to get into the habit of calling on students who volunteer to answer questions and allowing those who are shy, detached, or lacking in confidence to opt out of active participation in classroom discourse. This practice allows mental dropouts to evolve, and it no doubt contributes to physically dropping out as well. In a differentiated classroom, the value placed on the success of each student necessitates practices that are inclusive and engage each learner. One teacher signals this idea to her students by saying, "In here, nobody gets to be invisible."

There are two key goals to developing routines for calling on students:

- Make sure everyone in the class has both the opportunity and responsibility to speak.
- Develop a system that helps students make meaningful contributions to class discussions, conversations, or deliberations.

A high school teacher explains to her students that she feels her role in discussions is to prepare intriguing and important questions for the class to consider. "Your role," she says to her students, "is to be prepared to share your perspectives on the questions. Every one of you has something valuable to contribute to our thinking. I will call on you in ways that ensure each of you has a voice here." She uses three methods to call on students. In "Bag of Names," she writes the names of all her students on small slips of paper and collects them in a small lunch bag. She draws names from the bag and calls students randomly. She also uses a "Volunteers" approach in which she encourages students who want to make a contribution or a point to do so—an important time for students with advanced knowledge, strong opinions, or an itch to be heard. Finally, she calls for "New Voices"—students who have not spoken during Bag of Names or Volunteers. She reminds students of their responsibility to share their perspectives with the class, and students respond appropriately.

To ensure that all students participate—including those who are learning the language of the classroom, those who have not seen themselves (and who have not been seen) as smart, those who are reticent, and those who feel unprepared because of a lack of background experience—the teacher uses a variety of approaches that students come to understand and appreciate. Sometimes, she might "prime" a student for a question by saying, "In a minute, Josh, I'm going to ask your opinion about the benefits of the amendment for the development of the United States, but first, I want to hear from one more person about why it may have taken so long for the amendment to pass." She then calls on someone from the bag of names for the latter question, giving Josh, who responds more confidently with some thinking time, the opportunity to mentally prepare an answer for the question the teacher will ask him.

At another point, she calls on a student who does not know an answer or who does not have the vocabulary to express it. Seeing the student's hesitancy, she says, "Give me a word or phrase that comes to your mind when you think about the question." She then draws another name from the bag and says, "Please build on Annanji's idea." The second student then expands on the initial idea, and the teacher repeats this process with another student or two before returning to Annanji to say, "Let me repeat the question now, Annanji, and you tell us what you think is important to consider as we try to answer it." Inevitably, the hesitant student can provide an expanded response. Students become accustomed to building on one another's ideas and sometimes say, "I'll say what I'm thinking now, but maybe some other people in the class could build on my idea."

Figure 6.1

Methods to Call on Students Equitably

Strategy	Explanation
Name Sticks	For younger students, draw student names (written on tongue depressors or popsicle sticks) from a cup to have them answer questions or share ideas in the classroom. Ask the question(s) first so that all students must think of a response before they know who will be asked to answer. When a question has a student stumped, he or she is allowed to ask for help from a classmate.
Spinner System	Use a system of assigning students to table groups (usually with four students to a group), and classify the groups by color and each student (within a group) by number. Use spinners to determine the color and number for a variety of tasks. For example, student 3 from the orange group might be asked to respond. If spinners are not available as part of your instructional tools, homemade versions are easy to construct. They are also readily available in children's board games.
Baseball Cards	Students from upper elementary and middle school classrooms are asked to create a baseball card that has their picture on the front (these can be school pictures or photos that are taken in class) and "statistics" that reveal something about the student (e.g., family information, hobbies, goals) on the back. Use the cards to learn more about each student and to randomly call on students to respond. This can be done in a variety of exciting ways, such as how a professional card player would draw a card.
Computer-Generated Names	A random, computer-generated list of student names is quite easy to use and motivating for students. This can be used at any grade level, but it is especially helpful for secondary teachers who often teach many students and for whom computer-generated lists can be a time-saver.

Figure 6.1 provides some ways to call on students to ensure that everyone in the class has both the opportunity and responsibility to be a contributor to class discussions.

Working in Groups

In order to realize that working in groups is complicated, all we need to do is watch school boards, city councils, state or national legislatures, or teacher committees in action. On many levels, it's easier to be a soloist than a member of an ensemble. Nevertheless, most experts tell us that collaboration and the use of collective intelligence to solve problems are skills our students must develop if they are to be prepared for life in the world beyond school (e.g., Cookson, 2009; Wagner, 2008; Zhao, 2009).

Students can learn to work effectively in groups in the same ways that they learn mathematical operations, the skills of a sport, or proficiency in singing—

with instruction, guidance, and practice. In other words, teachers need to teach students how to work in groups effectively. They also need to establish opportunities for students to work together in meaningful and productive ways on assignments that are important and engaging. It's in this context that students can develop and polish their skills of collaboration.

As you develop procedures, guidelines, and routines for group work, and as you design the work groups will do, consider (and make sure your students understand) the following skills for effective group work.

- Be prepared for the work of the group.
- Understand the parameters of the group's work.
- Make a plan to accomplish the work of the group, including creating an effective division of labor that matches individual strengths with key goals.
- Evaluate the progress of the group toward achieving goals, and adjust plans as needed.
- Listen to one another carefully.
- Be empathetic when group members have difficulty.
- Help one another solve problems.
- Make and respond to suggestions.

Design group tasks that support both meaningful collaboration and student achievement of desired outcomes. These tasks are characterized by hallmarks of high-quality work, such as

- Students understand the task goals.
- The task tightly aligns with learning goals (i.e., it leads students directly to what they should know, understand, and be able to do).
- Most students find the task interesting.
- Students understand what's expected of them as individuals in support of the group's work.
- The task requires genuine collaboration in order to achieve shared understanding (i.e., it cannot be done more effectively by an individual or subset of students in the group than by the group as a whole).
- The task requires an important contribution from each group by drawing on the strengths of the individuals in the group.
- The task is demanding of the group and its members.

- The pace of the work is brisk (but not rigid), and students feel the need to remain focused on the work.

- The group is responsible for a shared understanding of the content of the work and group processes.

- Opportunities exist for teacher or peer coaching.

- In-process quality checks support productive use of student time and strong outcomes.

- Students understand what to do next when they complete their work at a high level of quality.

Provide a "way out" for students who cannot succeed in a group at a given time. In other words, a student should not have to continue working in a group context if it becomes apparent that the individual or the group will suffer as a result. Some students have ongoing struggles with social skills or emotional volatility, and others simply have the occasional bad day. If group members work responsibly to support one another and a particular student continues to have or create difficulty working in the group, talk with that student privately and ask him or her to work independently (in a different part of the room) on a meaningful task for the remainder of the group work time. This should not be done punitively or with anger, but rather simply explain that working with the group is not productive at the moment, and an alternative seems like a better idea. Later, talk with the student again to see if he or she can identify the cause of friction with the group, and determine some ways to address the issue. Work with the student to help him or her reenter the group successfully when the time is right. This may mean talking with the group about its processes, closely monitoring the group to suggest adjustments, or making it possible for the student to work with the group for shorter periods of time (so he or she can experience success with the group but not remain long enough for problems to arise).

The goal should be to work patiently with the student and to develop the skills necessary for him or her to work more effectively with peers. When this is not possible, however, the student should understand when and how to separate from the group—or you should intervene as unobtrusively as possible to make that happen—to avoid escalating problems and creating long-lasting difficulties. If necessary, it's fine to say to the class (which, no doubt, is keenly aware of any problems a student may have with group or individual interactions), "You know, some of us find it very challenging to spell words correctly. Some of us have a hard time writing. Some of us find it really tough to memorize things. Some of us find it difficult to work in group settings. That's okay, because we all have the ability to get better at the things we find to be difficult. I'll ask you to work hard on the things that are difficult for you, and I hope you'll try to help one another with challenges as well. I'm confident every one of us can succeed."

Managing Noise

It's important for students to talk with one another at appropriate times in order to learn together. It's also easy for conversations among students (who are completely focused on their work) to escalate, simply because 25 to 40 voices in a relatively small space can be overwhelming. The goal in an orderly, flexible classroom is not "no noise" but rather "productive noise." Making noise work in favor of learning—rather than against it—is a maintenance issue in classes where students work collaboratively. However, it need not be a problem so much as a detail to which the teacher and students attend, such as keeping pencils sharpened or making sure materials are straight and stored properly. Think about the following ideas as you develop routines for handling noise in the classroom.

Clarify student expectations. Be sure students understand that you want them to work with you to monitor their conversations. This helps them work together effectively and successfully.

Place a value on silent work. Teach students what it means to work silently, and enforce this rule by routinely asking them to do so. It's sometimes helpful to introduce activities that require silence very early in the year so students develop a point of comparison and know how to transition to silence when needed. If the whole class finds it difficult to maintain silence, be sure to ask students to work silently for brief periods that are slightly shorter than the length of time they can remain silent. This will allow students to successfully work silently from the outset. You can then gradually extend the lengths of silent work expected of them.

Define acceptable noise limits. Develop indicators of or terms for various noise levels that you and the students can use with mutual understanding. Then translate them into a routine that establishes and monitors classroom noise. Consider the following examples.

- Remind young students to reduce their voice levels by saying, "Boys and girls, give me five." Students then stop what they were doing, open their hands, and bend their fingers toward their palms as you count down from five—pinkie first, ring finger second, middle finger third, and thumb fourth. With their index fingers extended, say "one" as students put their fingers in front of their closed lips. The few seconds of silence, along with the established quiet signal, remind students to begin working again very quietly. Alternatively, you could say, "Boys and girls, VW." Students stop their conversations and follow suit as you alternately hold up two and three fingers, switching between a *V* and a *W.* The students should understand that "VW" means "voices, whisper." Again, the reminder has the desired effect.

• Post a stoplight in elementary classrooms. Green represents noise at a conversational level, yellow is a whisper, and red is complete silence. An arrow beside the appropriate level for a particular task helps students get ready to transition into a new task. If the noise level rises above the appropriate level, say, "Eyes up front, everyone. Stoplight check." Likewise, a "noiseometer," made to look like a thermometer, can also indicate noise levels from "acceptable" to "uncomfortable" to "unacceptable."

• When voices rise beyond a comfortable level, say (in a slightly raised voice), "If you can hear me, clap once." A few students will likely respond, but the sound gets the attention of others. In a softer voice, say, "If you can hear me, clap twice." Continue this pattern, increasing the number of claps and reducing voice volume, until the count of four or five. Students are inevitably all listening and clapping by two or three.

• Designate four categories of voice levels—"mute button" (i.e., no sound), "six-inch voices" (i.e., someone standing or sitting more than six inches away from you cannot hear what you are saying), "work voices" (i.e., appropriate, conversational levels), and "playground/hall voices" (i.e., unacceptably loud levels). Students should learn to shift to "six inch voices" or to push the "mute button" when reminded to do so.

• Designate one student in each group whose role is to monitor the voice level of the group and give reminders as necessary.

• Remind students of appropriate voice levels as you walk around the classroom, and compliment groups when they talk at the designated level.

Allow students to block out distracting noise. Sometimes, there are students in a class who are very sensitive to noise and are distracted even when classmates are talking at acceptable levels. It can therefore be beneficial for those students to use headsets with "cuffs" that sit around the ears and help dampen noise. Similarly, inexpensive ear plugs (available in drug stores and airports) can help students who need to reduce or eliminate surrounding noise. In the latter instance, keep sets of assigned ear plugs for those students in a designated place in the room.

Getting Help

Students often learn to see the teacher as their primary, if not exclusive, source of help in the classroom when they work independently or in small groups. Although teachers will always need to be key players in a classroom support system, they have little time to do anything but dart around the room and put out fires when they are the predominate source of help. When this is the case, there's no time to teach individual students or small groups of students, no time to conduct systematic observations of students, no time to observe patterns in the work habits of individuals or groups. As a result, the teacher performs functions that someone else could handle and gives up on roles only the teacher can play. When students learn routines for getting help while they work independently and in small groups, the teacher is free to do targeted teacher and strategic observation. Consider the following ideas as you develop routines to guide students in getting help.

Develop clear directions. Invest time in developing very clear directions—whether written or oral—that you will ask students to follow. They should be brief, use accessible vocabulary, proceed in a step-by-step manner, and not skip any steps. To avoid as much confusion as possible, the directions should be formulated to anticipate ways in which students might misinterpret them.

Teach students to be active listeners. Make a game or contest out of seeing who can summarize directions or repeat the last thing you said. As they become conscious listeners, students are much better able to help themselves know how to proceed with a task. Many questions come from students who don't listen well in the first place because they know you will repeat the directions if they didn't hear them the first time.

Make sure students know when to ask for help. Teach students when it's all right to come to you for help, and when it's not. In a differentiated classroom, there will be times when the teacher is off-limits. Among them are times when you are working with individuals or small groups and when students are making transitions from one task or position to another. In the former instance, it's important to have uninterrupted time to work with individuals and small groups. In the latter instance, it's useful to be unencumbered to monitor student movement around the room and to make sure students settle in to their new work places smoothly. In general, it contributes to "clutter" in the classroom if students can get up and approach you at any time for questions, for supplies, or to turn in papers. For this reason, alternative routines for getting help are valuable.

Make sure students know when to ask their peers for help. Likewise, students should recognize when it's all right to ask peers for help, when it's not, and how to ask for help appropriately. In general, classmates are excellent sources of help, and when students learn to pull together and help one another, both collegiality and community develop.

Use "question chips." Give each student one or two poker chips at the beginning of the day. When they ask you for help, they must pay one chip. Once their chips are gone, they have no choice but to rely on their peers for help (questions to classmates are "free"). They learn very quickly that, most of the time, a classmate can be an excellent source of help. It's important to not be too rigid with the chips. Continue to move among students as they work, asking if they need help (questions that you pose to students are also "free"). The goal is not to deprive students of the assistance they need, but to expand the sources of help they feel comfortable drawing upon.

Administer "first aid." In elementary classrooms, it can be helpful to have a "first aid" area on the classroom wall. Beneath the area, students' names are printed on large pieces of cardboard made to look like bandages. Students who try to get assistance from two classmates but still need your help should post their bandages on the "first aid" board. Check the board often as you move from group to group so you know who needs help quickly.

Figure 6.2 provides additional examples of routines to ensure that students get timely help when you are not immediately available to help.

Helping Students Transition

In a differentiated classroom, students regularly move among whole-class, small-group, and independent work. These shifts often include different student groupings, the need for different materials, and the necessity to move to various parts of the room. Although any student of any age is capable of making these transitions smoothly, they also have the capacity to generate a good deal of disruption and distraction as they move between tasks and places. Transition routines are important from the very beginning of the year so students always understand how

Figure 6.2

Methods to Ensure Students Receive Help When Needed

Strategy	Explanation
Expert of the Day	One of many jobs students might have in a classroom is to play the role of "Expert of the Day." Students in this role are the designated "go to" person on a particular topic, assignment, or procedure. Every student knows that he or she will have a turn in this role, so they all understand they are capable of helping others. Teachers of young children sometimes use visors with "Ask Me" written on the bill. Teachers of older students generally designate Experts of the Day orally or on the board.
Colored Cups	Colored drinking cups are placed on student tables when groups are working together. Students use the cups to indicate the status of their work. A green cup on top of the stack means "Our group is working well and doesn't need help." A yellow cup means "We think we're OK, but we're not absolutely sure." A red cup means "We're stuck and can't go on." The cups indicate where immediate help is most important. It's also useful to note patterns in the cups. When groups never need help, it may mean the work is too easy for the group. When one group often has a red cup on top of the stack, it might be that the work is too difficult for them and more differentiation is necessary.
Question Sign	Question cards are an individual signal students use to indicate a need for assistance. Students fold a large index card in the middle and draw a large question mark on both sides of the card. They then stand the sign like a placard if they have used other sources of help but are still uncertain of how to move ahead with their work. The cards efficiently signal where help is needed.
Mini-Workshops	Mini-workshops are typically teacher initiated and result from observations made while moving around the room, such as noticing that several students have difficulty with the same skill or have a similar misunderstanding. You might say, "As I'm looking at your work, I see that several of you are a bit fuzzy on how to reduce a fraction. If you're not really confident of how to do that, meet with me on the floor in the front of the room." Students who need help benefit from a quick review and an opportunity to ask questions before returning to their work. You can also use mini-workshops to help individual students as necessary. It's possible for students to request a mini-workshop independently if they realize several of them are struggling with a particular skill or idea.

they can contribute to orderly transitions. The following suggestions should be useful as you plan routines for classroom transitions.

Clarify expectations. Discuss with students what will be necessary to enable a large number of them to move from place to place in the classroom, get supplies, and settle in to do work effectively. They should be able to identify elements such as walking quietly, moving quickly from place to place in the most direct way, limiting talking during transitions, paying attention to where they need to be and what they need to take with them (rather than being concerned about where classmates are going), and getting seated as soon as possible.

Create a time challenge. Time students as they shift locations early in the year. Challenge them to make transitions as quickly as they can without running or getting in one another's way. Students quickly learn that they are expected to move efficiently, and they retain that pattern throughout the year. Post the "best time" or a timer on the board to motivate students to make transitions quickly.

Organize materials logically. Store materials and supplies in locations around the perimeter of the room so students can retrieve and return items with minimal movement through the center of the room (where peers are working). Students quickly learn to walk around the perimeter to get what they need rather than walking across the room.

Designate a "Supply Student." When students will be using a common set of materials in a group, it is efficient for one student to get the materials for the entire group during a transition rather than have each student get the materials. Likewise, it's generally more efficient to have one student per group retrieve materials while the rest of the group is working. This same student could be responsible for asking questions (at the appropriate time) or having work checked. This reduces the amount of traffic and potential chaos caused by multiple students from each group moving around the room or vying for your attention. Finally, it often makes sense for one student per group to return materials, supplies, and student folders as work ends and students transition again. Also consider assigning one or two students from the class to do a quick tour of the classroom to make sure that seating areas are clear and clean and that all materials and supplies are in the right places at the end of transitions.

Post alternative floor plans. Create multiple room arrangement charts, and post them on a bulletin board. For example, they might be labeled "Discussion Format," "Current Events Format," "Seminar Format," and "Team Format." All four charts should include all of the room's furniture in varied arrangements. With guidance, students practice moving the furniture into the different arrangements several times (quickly and quietly), and they learn where to move their "home base" seats to accommodate each of the arrangements. Within a very short time, students will be able to change the entire room configuration with precision and speed. This provides tremendous flexibility in using classroom space, and students become proud of their "drill team" moves.

Managing Time

It's never the case in any classroom that students all finish an assignment at exactly the same moment—or that all students need exactly the same amount of time to achieve mastery in a particular area. A differentiated classroom differs from others only in that it recognizes and accommodates "ragged time." Such accommodations exist on two levels—one focuses on the need for flexibility in the short term, the other in the longer term. In the short term, *student* routines are needed for what students should do when they complete a task before the teacher "calls time" or when a student needs a bit more time to complete an assignment. In the longer term, the *teacher* must have routines that allow forward and backward teaching at the same time. Think about the following strategies as you develop student and teacher routines for managing time.

Use anchor activities from very early in the year. An anchor activity is a task (or a set of tasks) to which students move when they complete an assignment. Figure 6.3 lists characteristics of quality anchor activities. Create a routine for moving from an assignment to an anchor activity. Should they check the quality of their completed assignment with you? With a peer? Where should the completed work go? Where are anchor options located in the room? May any student choose any anchor task? Do students sit where they were previously seated while working on the anchor activity? How should they work with the anchor task so that they are not distracting peers? Is there any time limit or expectation with any of the anchor options? Is there a procedure for getting help with an anchor task? What should they do with completed work—turn it in, put it in a work folder?

Add to the list of options gradually. Start the year with a small set of anchor activity options, and add new options as students become familiar with them and as the curriculum expands. Students will be able to suggest or create their own anchor activities as the year progresses.

Figure 6.3
Characteristics of High-Quality Anchor Activities

❏ Activities are focused on essential learning goals (not tangential or trivial).
❏ Activities are engaging (not rote practice).
❏ Activities address a broad range of student interests and help make content relevant for students from a variety of backgrounds.
❏ Activities address a broad range of readiness needs and vary from concrete to abstract, structured to open-ended, and simple to complex.
❏ Activities allow for a variety of ways of taking in and expressing ideas that address a broad range of learning profile needs.
❏ Activities are presented with clear directions so students know what to do, what the final product should be, how they will know when they are finished, and what to do with the work they generate.
❏ Activities incorporate a monitoring system so the teacher and students can recognize the level of quality produced and any need for adjustment.

Do not grade anchor activities. Look at the work students are doing to provide brief feedback and encouragement. The clear and persistently reinforced ethic of a differentiated classroom simply needs to be "there are so many interesting things to learn, it's never acceptable to just stop working." When a student finishes one assignment, he or she should automatically start an anchor activity as the next assignment. Students should understand that you've designed anchor activities to be interesting, accessible, and able to increase their sense of competence. Invite students to suggest their own ideas for anchor activities. You may want to give students a "mark" (not a grade) for how well they work with these tasks as a mechanism for discussing their work habits and habits of mind.

Explain the ground rules for extra time. Determine and share with students conditions under which it's likely for them to get additional time to work on an assignment after you "call time" for the class. For example, if you observe that a student worked very diligently on the task but simply needs a bit more time, it makes sense to provide that time. It may also be important to give a student extra time to work on a task if he or she is eager to pursue the topic in greater depth. On the other hand, it may not be wise to give a student additional time to complete a piece of work if he or she wasted time or didn't focus on the task. Still, it's necessary to look beyond the surface. It may be that the student has enduring attention problems or that he or she didn't focus on the work because it was much too difficult or much too easy. You want to provide time for students to finish the work if it seems beneficial to do so without fostering a sense that if they lollygag, they'll get a reprieve. On extended assignments, such as projects or authentic assessments, a "petition for extended time" may be useful with older learners. The petition should make the case for an extension, and this process tends to signal to students the difference between *needing* more time to achieve high-quality work and *wanting* more time because of procrastination. Figure 6.4 provides an example of a petition created for secondary students, and an example for elementary school students is included in the Teacher's Toolkit.

Teachers in differentiated classrooms need their own routines for handling the inevitability that some students will be ready to move ahead in content before others, that some students will need to linger on a topic in order to develop key competencies and understandings, and that some students will need to revisit content from earlier years to move ahead effectively with the current year's content goals. In other words, teachers in effectively differentiated classrooms learn to teach forward and backward at the same time. Consider the following strategies as you think about these scenarios.

Figure 6.4
Petition for an Extension of Time on a Project

Student's Name: _____

Date: _____

Project: _____

In the space below, please make your case for requesting an extension of time on this piece of work. Remember that extensions will only be granted in cases where (1) there is good evidence that you used your time on the project effectively, (2) you made sure the teacher was aware of your progress throughout the assignment period, and (3) there is solid evidence that extended time will allow you to develop a product of very high quality.

Length of the extension you are requesting: _____

Decision of the teacher: _____

Teacher comments:

Develop procedures for providing meaningful challenge. Figure 6.5 indicates some strategies teachers can use to challenge advanced learners who have mastered the content that most of the class still needs to study. With these strategies in place, students recognize that there is a consistent plan for their growth, and they don't develop expectations for "success" with little effort. Be sure you work with these students to provide them with important teacher connections, to support them when work is difficult (which should frequently be the case), and to provide feedback on their work. Highly able students need teacher support and attention as much as any other student does—especially if their work is appropriately challenging. When possible, coplanning or coteaching with a specialist in gifted education can help you understand how to develop student work at an advanced level of challenge.

Figure 6.5
Methods to Challenge Advanced Learners

Strategy	Explanation
Complex Applications of Content	An advanced learner may be challenged by using current knowledge, understanding, and skills in applications that are unfamiliar, abstract, or multifaceted. Asking these students to use multiple sets of skills simultaneously to address problems that don't have a ready solution can also be challenging. For example, Trey's 3rd grade teacher worked with his school's resource teacher for advanced learners to find a real-world math problem for him to pursue. Trey had to use addition, subtraction, and multiplication, in addition to basic geometry, to solve the problem. Although he had studied those concepts in class, he seldom had to use multiple operations at once. Ultimately, Trey became excited about thinking his way through an approach to math that was new to him.
Advanced and Extended Resources	Challenge can result from a student's use of advanced resources such as books, websites, or contacts with experts to gain a deeper understanding of a topic. For example, employees at a local fish hatchery suggested some Internet and print resources that 7th grader Luis could use to learn about endangered fish species in his area. Because Luis had an advanced level of knowledge about several topics in his science unit, his teacher encouraged him to develop a project examining potential ways to protect the species and to offer his solutions and suggestions to an environmental agency. The project lasted for several months, and Luis worked on it in lieu of two differentiated unit projects completed by most of his classmates.
Focus on Interest	Some students may be advanced in one content area but not be particularly intrigued by that area. In such instances, students can learn about an area of personal interest with time that they can "buy" because of early mastery of the required content. For example, Matt learned math very quickly in 5th grade and often needed much less time than his peers to master a topic. Although he didn't find math particularly interesting, he was very eager to learn about anthropology. Matt and his teacher developed a long-term anthropology investigation that he would work on when he finished a math unit early.
Making Connections	Students often study subjects in school in a disconnected way. Therefore, it can be exciting and challenging for them to discover connections across content areas. For example, Jana was a very strong reader and also knew a lot about social studies. Her teacher developed an ongoing anchor activity for her in which she read novels and biographies about the time periods and people she and her classmates were studying in school. She kept a journal about connections she saw across her readings (in response to questions posed by her teacher and based on her own insights). She worked on the anchor activity when she mastered social studies content rapidly, when she finished any class task early, and when there was a social studies or language arts homework assignment her teacher felt she didn't need to complete.
Moving On	Advanced learners sometimes have great talent in one content area and a hunger to learn more about it. In such instances, it may be that the only meaningful challenge is for students to move ahead at their own pace. This can be accomplished by providing appropriately leveled text materials and support with those materials. Sometimes, a learner may need to work with students in a more advanced grade level in a particular subject, and the school will need to work with the student and his or her parents to examine the pros and cons of advancing the student's grade level. The goal should be to find the best possible source of challenge for that student at a particular time. Results should be monitored carefully and modified if necessary.

Develop procedures for "buying time." Struggling students will occasionally need to continue working with current tasks after other students have completed their work. You may also need to guide these students to develop essential knowledge, understanding, and skills from previous years. You must first identify the knowledge, understanding, and skills that are truly essential to the student's continued growth and have not been developed. By focusing on genuinely non-negotiable knowledge that the student must master and eliminating what would be nice to know if there were time, it is usually possible to identify a substantial amount of time for "working backwards" on gaps in knowledge from previous years while still helping the student progress with current goals. Figure 6.6 suggests some mechanisms for focusing students' attention on nonnegotiable knowledge,

Figure 6.6
Methods to "Buy Time" for Struggling Students

Strategy	Explanation
Learning Contracts, Menus, Centers, and Computer Programs	Instructional strategies such as these are designed to help teachers provide varied work for students around common topics, skills, or concepts. A student who needs additional practice with academic vocabulary in science, for example, may have a contract or learning menu focused on science vocabulary, whereas other students will focus on different content. These approaches also allow teachers to incorporate both current and past content into student assignments.
Regular Individual and Small-Group Instruction	It's important to plan consistent time to work with individuals or small groups who have learning gaps or who learn content with difficulty. This is a particularly efficient means of understanding students' needs, providing targeted instruction, and assessing student progress.
Alternative Homework Assignments	Continually attempting homework that is beyond a student's reach leads to frustration and confusion. If a particular homework assignment is inappropriate for a student, it is much wiser to give that student an assignment that helps him or her make progress with past learning gaps.
Scaffolded Assignments	It is often possible to create a scaffolded version of an assignment that other students can complete with little or no support. Scaffolding can include step-by-step directions, examples, "watch out for" warnings where students might get confused, hints written in the columns, content that is rewritten in more straightforward language, recorded directions or resource materials, and the inclusion of both English and a student's first language.
Double-Dipping	It is sometimes helpful for elementary students to work with a content area more than once a day. For example, a student might meet with two reading groups to practice decoding or comprehension skills. Some secondary school students can be placed in two periods of the same subject—in one, the teacher differentiates the content for students, and in the other, the teacher reinforces the goals of the first class by teaching the ideas in a different way, probing student thinking for understanding and misunderstanding, and focusing on particularly complex skills. In the latter instance, the two class periods must be very tightly coordinated and aligned.

understanding, and skills, both past and current. Whichever strategies you use for this purpose, students must still be asked to do essential, proactively planned, sequentially offered, and consistently monitored work. These principles are imperative at all grade levels and in all content areas. Sometimes, coplanning or coteaching with a learning specialist can yield considerable benefits for both you and your students.

Keeping Track

Teachers in all classrooms have the responsibility to monitor student proficiency in relation to designated learning goals. A differentiated classroom varies only in that the teacher assumes students may sometimes work with different goals at different times or for varied lengths of time. It's not difficult to know who has mastered what in a differentiated classroom as long as the teacher is clear about the essential learning goals and has a system for monitoring student growth toward those goals. With a clear scope and sequence or delineation of what students should learn, a teacher can monitor a particular student's progress toward established goals, even if the student is working with different materials, on a different timetable, or with tasks at different levels of difficulty. Figure 6.7 provides an example of a record-keeping system used in an elementary classroom to monitor student growth in the key elements of reading. The sheets are alphabetized by student name, and each form is accompanied by several blank sheets of paper on which the teacher attaches or writes observations obtained in a variety of contexts. Even when students work with varied assignments, the teacher is able to readily monitor their progress toward common goals. Figure 6.8 presents a similar example at a secondary level.

An Important Reminder

School is a place of learning for students and teachers alike. Even though every procedure and routine in this book is valuable in providing structures that allow flexible teaching and learning, it makes no sense to teach students of any age to understand and implement all of them at once. Your goal should be to begin with the most fundamental routines and introduce new ones as they are needed and as students are ready for them—polishing and revising as you go.

Similarly, teachers who are new to leading and managing a differentiated classroom need to see themselves as learners, too. For most teachers, it's overwhelming

Figure 6.7
Record of Reading Progress

Student: _____

1st Assessment Date: _____

2nd Assessment Date: _____

3rd Assessment Date: _____

4th Assessment Date: _____

Elements of Reading	#1	#2	#3	#4
Reading Strategies				
✓ skips unknown words and reads on				
✓ guesses what the word might be				
✓ starts over and reads the whole sentence				
✓ derives meaning from the pictures (or words)				
✓ uses beginning letter as a clue				
✓ asks for help				
Phonemic Awareness				
Concepts of Print				
Phonics				
Word Recognition				
Fluency				
Comprehension				

Teacher Comments:

#1	#2	#3	#4

Figure 6.8

Checklist of Writing Skills and Competencies

Student: _____ Date: _____ Evaluation: _____

Content and Expression
- ❑ Main idea is evident and appropriate.
- ❑ Details support key idea/argument.
- ❑ Descriptive details engage reader and extend ideas.
- ❑ Shows understanding of topic.
- ❑ Shows insight about topic.

Organization
- ❑ Effective title.
- ❑ Introduction establishes purpose.
- ❑ Logical flow of paragraphs.
- ❑ Logical flow of ideas within paragraphs.
- ❑ Effective transitions to guide reader.
- ❑ Conclusion summarizes/emphasizes key idea(s).

Style
- ❑ Word choice is appropriate for audience/topic.
- ❑ Word choice is precise for purpose.
- ❑ Vocabulary is varied and engaging.
- ❑ Sentences are complete.
- ❑ Sentences are clear.
- ❑ Sentence length varies.
- ❑ Sentence structure is varied.

Mechanics
- ❑ Subjects & verbs agree.
- ❑ Verb tenses are consistent.
- ❑ Subjects & objects agree.
- ❑ Plurals are used correctly.
- ❑ Capitalization is used correctly.
- ❑ End punctuation is correct.
- ❑ Commas are used correctly.
- ❑ Apostrophes are used correctly.
- ❑ Spelling is correct.

Teacher Comments:

to think about planning, implementing, and supervising all of these routines at once. Teachers should accord themselves the privilege of learning, just as they do their students. Choose one or two routines you feel would be helpful to move your teaching forward. Plan for them carefully. Implement them when you feel ready. Study the results as you go. Take time to polish and become comfortable with one routine or set of routines before you take on others.

If you pace yourself in a persistent pattern of growth, you will eventually not be able to recall what it was like to teach any other way. Not surprisingly, your students will learn the routines more rapidly at that point. In the meantime, however, be patient with yourself. Be a learner. Take one step, then another. Figure things out along with your students. Don't be afraid to stumble from time to time. Most importantly, enjoy the journey.

7

Yes, But...
Common Sticking Points About Differentiation

In a real sense all life is interrelated. All men are caught in an inescapable network of mutuality, tied in a single garment of destiny. Whatever affects one directly affects all indirectly. I can never be what I ought to be until you are what you ought to be, and you can never be what you ought to be until I am what I ought to be. This is the interrelated structure of reality.

—Dr. Martin Luther King, Jr.

Human beings seldom cozy up to the need to make big changes in their lives—and teachers are human beings. In the face of evidence that we would fare better if we exercised more, we often assert that we simply don't have the time. Faced with the need to save for a rainy day, many of us declare that there simply is no margin in our budgets. Presented with evidence that student-focused teaching has multiple benefits for students and teachers, many teachers have a ready and substantial list of "yes, but . . ." statements.

- I can't differentiate instruction because I have to cover the standards for everyone.
- I can't differentiate instruction because the standardized test is not differentiated.
- I can't differentiate instruction because I'm already too busy and have absolutely no extra time for planning.
- I can't differentiate instruction because I teach too many students.
- I can't differentiate instruction because I have only one textbook.
- I can't differentiate instruction because my classroom is too small.
- I can't differentiate instruction because it won't prepare students for college.
- I can't differentiate instruction because parents won't accept it.

The reality is, of course, that most of these excuses are easily addressed.

I can't differentiate instruction because I have to cover the standards for everyone. Differentiation is an instructional approach and does not dictate curriculum, although it does suggest—based on much research and visible evidence—that student learning is far more durable and purposeful when the curriculum is rich with meaning. The primary goal of differentiation, however, is to help teachers develop and use multiple pathways for students to learn whatever they teach.

I can't differentiate instruction because the standardized test is not differentiated. Research clearly indicates that students will typically perform better on standardized tests when they have had the opportunity to learn in preferred modes, even if the test is not in their preferred mode (e.g., Grigorenko, Jarvin, & Sternberg, 2002; Sternberg, Torff, & Grigorenko, 1998). This is true because they learned the content better and because they entered the testing situation with greater confidence in themselves as learners. There's little logic to teaching students in a way that's awkward for them just so they will be "prepared" for a test that is awkward for them.

I can't differentiate instruction because I'm already too busy and have absolutely no extra time for planning. The idea is not to plan everything the way you always have and then plan differentiation on top of that. Rather, it is to plan instruction in a differentiated fashion from the outset. In addition, it's essential for teachers to pace themselves and move into new ways of thinking about teaching and learning at a level that produces growth and change without being overwhelming.

I can't differentiate instruction because I teach too many students. This comment is made variously by teachers with 20 to 35 students in their classrooms. The number of students does not seem to dictate the response. In fact, we've heard this excuse from teachers whose enrollment was as low as 12 or 15. We've also worked with teachers who regularly differentiate with more than 40 students in their classrooms. Would it be beneficial if the teacher–student ratio was lower? It's hard not to advocate for that, yet we regularly see teachers with reduced class sizes who continue to teach just as they did in settings with more students.

I can't differentiate instruction because I have only one textbook. There are countless materials other than the textbook. Usually, teachers have access to old or otherwise unused textbooks that contain material on the same topics as a current text but are written at different readability levels. The Internet throws open the doors in terms of readiness, interest, and even learning profile options. Media specialists are also valuable resources for matching materials to student needs.

I can't differentiate instruction because my classroom is too small. It would be great to teach in a spatially generous setting, but many of us don't have that luxury. Again, a small room size doesn't seem to discourage teachers who mean to differentiate instruction—although those teachers would doubtless love to have a larger room—and a larger room does not seem to be an automatic catalyst for student-focused instruction.

I can't differentiate instruction because it won't prepare students for college. If students were developmentally ready for college at 12 or even 16, we would send them. However, they are not ready. Effective differentiation should absolutely prepare students for higher education by ensuring that they learn the content, habits of mind, academic skills, and self-awareness necessary for continuing learning. Differentiation should always prepare students for the next chapter of their lives.

I can't differentiate instruction because parents won't accept it. Few parents recoil at the idea of a teacher who genuinely cares about the growth of their children and who is willing to invest in making sure students have the most productive year possible. This is what differentiation aims to do.

These "yes, but . . ." excuses are both common and predictable. They are a safety net in the face of a call to disrupt the generally comfortable routines we've established. To the degree that we can cling to them, we are justified in our sense that this "differentiation thing" is impractical—at least in our own classrooms. Nevertheless, many teachers who initially subscribe to a "yes, but . . ." excuse continue to watch their students and grow increasingly uncomfortable in the face of student frustration and stagnation. Those teachers finally take the risk and implement student-focused approaches in their classroom, and they often have two realizations. First, their students are the beneficiaries of their efforts. Second, addressing their students' needs wasn't nearly as forbidding as they had assumed it would be.

Incrementally (but steadily), these teachers learn to be responsive to the students they teach, and positive student outcomes encourage continued teacher development. Somewhere in this process, the excuses cease to serve a purpose and become an artifact of the past. In other words, propelled by a sense of necessity and nurtured by a sense of accomplishment, many teachers answer their own concerns through increasingly effective practices.

Not all "yes, but . . ." statements are excuses that typify an early response to change, however. Some are more complex and confounding. They persist even as teachers make changes toward effective differentiation in their classrooms. Two of the more challenging concerns involve particularly difficult students or teaching contexts and grading in a differentiated classroom. This final chapter will provide some thoughts and guidance on these two areas, both of which have implications for leading and managing a differentiated classroom. The two areas of concern are (1) implementing differentiation with students whose behavior is particularly challenging and (2) grading and differentiation.

But My Students Are Different

A number of teachers who genuinely desire to provide all of their students with the opportunity to access excellence and maximize their capacities look at their students and fear that some, many, or all of them can't handle the sort of flexible classroom that differentiation advocates. In essence, their response is something like "This would be wonderful, but I don't think you know the students I teach." The comment is not so much a dismissive "yes, but . . ." as it is a real sense that at least some portion of their students are not now capable of making decisions in their own self-interest, collaborating, or even following general guidelines for classroom civility.

It is important to note that virtually all teachers, at any given time, teach some students whose deprivation, anger, discouragement, disillusionment, alienation, frustration, or trauma are so great that it is difficult, if not impossible, for them to exhibit sustained contributions to a classroom community. Working with only a few of these students can be both challenging and gut-wrenching. Therefore, when a school or class is heavily populated with students whose lives are markedly off-course in one or more ways, the challenge is massive. There is no formula for teachers to follow in such settings. Rather, those classrooms demand the highest level of creativity from the teacher.

Still, there are principles that derive from both research and effective classroom practice to guide teachers who work with deeply disaffected students. We'll share a few of these principles in the following sections, including some general ideas about leading and guiding students whose lives are more difficult than a young person's should have to be and some guidelines for working with particular groups of students who may experience and create difficulties in the classroom.

In most classes, a majority of students are ready, willing, and able to be part of a learning community that is safe, welcoming, challenging, and supportive. There may be a few students who occasionally need additional support and reminders about procedures and guidelines. In such classes, the major challenge of leading and managing a classroom comes from one or a very few students who consistently push against the norms. In other classrooms, a majority of students do not affiliate with school, and the climb for teacher and students to achieve an orderly, flexible classroom is much steeper. The guidelines below are relevant to both contexts, but they will likely need to be implemented differently in the two contexts.

Don't lower your expectations for students. This is true in terms of behavior, classroom participation, and self-awareness as a learner exactly as it is true for cognitive outcomes. In regard to cognitive development, there is more than ample evidence that "remediating" students often further hobbles them (e.g., Allington, 1994; Cone, 2003; Finnian & Swanson, 2000; Hilliard, 2003; Hopfenberg & Levin, 2008). What they need to succeed are high expectations, acceleration that focuses on essential content to propel them forward, and support for the journey (Hopfenberg & Levin, 2008). In regard to meaningful participation in a classroom community, the same principle holds. Of all students in a school who need to learn the skills of academic self-awareness, peer collaboration, and community membership, those who need them most are those who are most alienated from the skills and the promise they represent. The path to achieving these skills with disaffected students is not easy, linear, straightforward, or quick. Nonetheless, you cannot serve disenfranchised students well unless you keep your eyes on the destination they need to reach and guide them steadily in that direction. In other words, we fail students when we look at what we believe they cannot do and lower our sights accordingly rather than look at what they need to do and continually try to lift them to that level.

Move slowly but persistently toward helping all students satisfy the same expectations. You may introduce ideas and routines more slowly in settings where many students exhibit challenging behavior. You may use the routines for briefer periods in a class or day. You may need to practice and model routines more frequently. You will doubtless have more false starts and disappointments along the way. What you should *not* do is accept the inevitability of a "tight-ship classroom," which, by its nature, communicates to students a lack of trust, eliminates the opportunity for students to engage with meaningful content, and deprives students of the chance to take control of their lives as learners.

Learn from the "warm demanders." It's often the case that students who are perennially disruptive in one class work quite well in another. The difference— particularly for students from low-income or African American backgrounds— is often that teachers in the classes where students are successful are "warm demanders" (Bondy & Ross, 2008; Ware, 2006). These teachers have two critical traits that may seem paradoxical but actually send important signals to students—especially those whose feelings about school are ambivalent or negative. First, the teachers are clear and unequivocal about expectations for behavior and work. Said otherwise, they don't put up with nonsense in the classroom. At the same time, however, they communicate to students their unconditional acceptance, unwavering belief in the each student's capacity to succeed, and full partnership in the goal of achieving success. In some cultures, parents are direct or even blunt in stating expectations and correcting misbehavior. For students from these backgrounds, such directness signals adult caring, and the "warm demander" fits that profile. Even students whose cultural expectations are for a more subdued form of communication may benefit from this clarity if they lack the internal structures necessary to make good judgments on their own behalf and if the demands are enveloped in the warmth of understanding and acceptance. Corita Kent, a graphic artist and author, once noted that a friend is someone who loves you just as you are and pays you the compliment of expecting you to become something better. Warm demanders do just that. In the process, they provide the external structures necessary to survive the moment and the guidance necessary to ultimately create internal structures that lead to self-direction.

Remember that young people will nearly always succeed if they can. Susan Craig (2008) and Ross Greene (2008) are two of many experts working with disaffected learners who remind us that it's more satisfying for young people to succeed than to fail. For this reason, most students will almost always do what is in their best interest if they have the skills to do so. Understanding this will help you think about an event or about the classroom in general from the student's perspective (and will help you avoid the trap of blaming the student). The two pertinent questions become "What academic and personal skills does this student need to develop to handle situations like this?" and "What can I do to help the student develop those skills?"

Invest heavily in trying to understand the cause of a student's misbehavior. A student may feel rejected by his or her peers, be frustrated by work that is out of reach, be bored on a daily basis, be hungry, see school as irrelevant to his or her life, find it impossible to sit and listen as much as is required, have a chronically ill family member, or be a victim of abuse or neglect. The gamut of possibilities is long and wide. It can be very helpful to understand the origin of counterproductive behavior in order to address it in a way that helps the student make sense of life rather than in a way that simply complicates life for the student. Greene reminds us that we don't need a diagnosis to address maladaptive behavior because a diagnosis doesn't yield any strategies for moving ahead (2008). Understanding the world from the student's point of view, however, can be immensely useful in helping you determine potentially beneficial next steps away from the problem and toward a constructive and long-lasting solution. From that point, you will be better positioned to help the student understand his or her behavior and to develop responses that are increasingly positive and productive.

Be proactive. Craig recalls being a young teacher who was focused on student accountability for behavior. One day she complained about a student who was regularly disruptive, and a colleague turned the tables and asked, "What can you change about your teaching practice to help this child be more successful?" (2008, p. 13) Recall some key tenets of this book and of differentiation. Students work more productively and successfully when the classroom feels safe, when they feel valued and supported, when the work teachers ask them to do is at an appropriate challenge level, when the work is personally and/or culturally relevant (and therefore interesting), and when there are opportunities to work in ways that are efficient for them. Working diligently to ensure that these conditions prevail in the classroom eliminates many problems. A veteran teacher once noted, "If the classroom system works for the kid, the kid generally quits working the system." However, be cognizant of patterns associated with a student's problematic behavior. You might increase the likelihood of a good outcome by seating the student in a particular place, providing step-by-step directions rather than a long paragraph, reminding the student of a goal he or she has set, assigning students to groups rather than risking the high likelihood that a particular student will be the last one chosen by a group, or allowing a student extra time to get organized before beginning a task. As in all aspects of teaching, planning for success and planning to avoid failure are powerful tools.

Pick your battles. Don't let smaller issues become flash points. Don't take negative behavior personally. Someone has to be the adult. There's a powerful moment in the movie *Stand and Deliver* when the teacher hands a book to a student only to have the student intentionally let the book fall to the floor. In a single gesture, the teacher picks the book up, opens it to the correct place, and continues to explain what the student needs to do. By refusing to allow the student's challenge to escalate, the teacher kept the focus on learning and maintained a positive interaction with the student. Keep the focus on learning whenever possible. Don't become a co-combatant with the student.

Don't be afraid to delay handling a tense situation. Of course, challenging behavior must be handled swiftly if student safety is an issue, but most of the time, it's both possible and wise to delay dealing with a behavior issue. You may simply say to a student (privately, if at all possible), "You're angry right now and it's difficult for you to concentrate on your work. I want to talk with you in a little while about this, but for right now, please write about how you're feeling in your journal." The immediate prescription for the student's next step will vary, of course, depending on his or her specific needs. The intention is to allow some time to think before you address the issue. Eliminating "heat" from a tense situation allows "light" to enter the picture.

Demonstrate empathy and respect to identify solutions to a problem. When the time is right, talk with the student privately and with the goal of finding a reasonable and acceptable solution to the problem. Cummings (2000) and Greene (2008) suggest beginning conversations with comments such as "I've noticed that you're not getting your homework done. Help me know what's up." "You're upset. Help me understand what you're thinking." "Talk about what happened earlier today when you were so angry with Charles. I need to understand how you were feeling." As the conversation progresses, guide it toward a problem-solving mode. Say something like "Let's figure out together how to address this. What do you think we can do to avoid this problem again?" Ultimately, the goal is to develop a series of steps that the student will take and you will support to eliminate, or at least minimize, the issue. Finally, you might end the conversation with a comment such as "Thank you for trusting me enough to tell me how you feel and for working with me to find a solution we can use." Along the way, it's important to be sure you both understand the problem that evoked the negative behavior and that there has been an opportunity to explore that problem and a potential solution in some depth. It may appear to some that this approach to maladaptive behavior is "too easy" on the student or that it "lets the student off the hook." In truth, this approach involves two elements central to differentiation: teaching and leadership. It helps students understand themselves better, develop the insights and skills necessary for continued personal and academic growth, and establish the kind of trust that's required to follow a leader to a better place. Discipline implies teaching and learning; punishment does not.

But Grading Requirements Don't Work with Differentiation

A discussion about grading and report cards seems somehow unrelated to classroom management, yet the classroom is a system and all of its elements are interdependent. Confusion about grading and differentiation is often not a dismissive "yes, but . . ." excuse. Rather, it can reflect genuine concern by teachers who work diligently to differentiate instruction but feel stymied by an apparent dissonance between the philosophy and goals of a differentiated classroom and those of grading. One teacher notes, "For nine weeks, I play the role of encourager, coach, and advocate. Then, on the last day of the nine weeks, I become the judge. It makes me feel like a fraud."

Teachers worry that grading, as schools typically practice it, seems punitive to students who struggle, that it rewards (and thus damages) students who are highly able and coast to success, and that it erodes teacher–student trust. Alternatively, they worry that, somehow, differentiation requires a teacher to "jiggle" grades so that struggling students receive elevated grades for hard work or lesser goals. They are then concerned that those grades will be misinterpreted by parents, teachers, and counselors at the next level of schooling. A colleague of ours, who is an expert in measurement and grading, often remarks that there is no problem inherent to reconciling grading and differentiation. Rather, she says, our grading practices are such a mess that they make everything a problem. All indications are that she's correct.

There is no inherent conflict in sound grading practices and the philosophy of differentiation. What teachers perceive to be issues typically arise from grading practices that are misaligned with best practice grading, not because best practice grading and differentiation are misaligned. The following principles and practices of grading are widely recommended by experts in the field of measurement and grading (e.g., Earl, 2003; Guskey, 2000; Guskey & Bailey, 2001; Marzano, 2000; O'Connor, 2002; Wiggins, 1993). As you read and think about them, consider the degree to which they support or undercut the goals of differentiation.

Grading is one moment in a long progression of assessment decisions. Perhaps the most common question about differentiation, asked by teachers from all grade levels, subject areas, and countries, is "Could you talk about assessment and differentiation?" We've learned to follow up with another question: "Explain what you mean by assessment." Nearly always, the answer is "Grading. I don't know how to grade differentiation." We must point out that grading and assessment are not synonyms. Assessment is the process of finding out where students are relative to key goals at a particular time. Grading is the periodic, somewhat public statement about a student's performance at designated intervals.

The nature of a teacher's decisions about assessment will affect grading. For many teachers, assessment means giving enough tests and recording enough grades so they can defend a student's final grade at the end of a marking period. This conception of assessment invites "gotcha teaching." Differentiation requires a different perspective. Preassessments and formative assessments become mechanisms to inform teacher planning, create a match between student needs and classroom instruction, and provide helpful feedback to students on their progress. Preassessments are never graded. Formative assessments are rarely graded, and then only with advance notice. In this way, ongoing assessment helps students understand learning goals and trace their progress toward those goals so that when graded assessments do occur, students are more likely to be prepared or to know how to prepare. Very different classroom climates result when a teacher sees the need for students to practice before they are "measured" and envisions the assessment process as largely informative, as opposed to as a series of grading opportunities.

Instruction should be differentiated. As teachers become more proficient with using what they learn about students to effectively address their readiness, interests, and learning profile needs, an array of benefits occur. Student achievement rises, and they begin to develop a more growth mind-set about themselves as learners—which contributes to their continuing investment in learning. Further, "grade trauma" diminishes not because a teacher awards extra points for trying hard, but because student achievement merits a higher grade.

Assessments should be differentiated. Effective assessments enhance the likelihood that students can truly demonstrate what they know, understand, and can do. Assessments that allow more than one way to demonstrate mastery are likely to serve more students better. In addition, when teachers use more than one—or more than one form of—summative assessment, more students are likely to have the opportunity to provide a more accurate accounting of what they have learned. Learning is multifaceted, and effective assessment plans take this reality into account.

Grading should stem from, not dictate, effective assessment practices. Too often in schools, the tail wags the dog in terms of grading. For example, we say, "I'm required to have at least 10 grades in my grade book each marking period, so I have to grade everything." We also say, "How can I document that I have provided specific feedback to students on their progress and guided them in setting personal goals for their work at least 10 times?" Finally, we might say, "I can't communicate anything but a single letter grade because the report card won't let me." In reality, we should ask, "What do I need to do in terms of reporting to benefit student achievement? What mechanisms, including but not limited to the report card, can support me in doing that?"

Grades should be based on clear and specific learning goals. When a teacher can clearly articulate precisely what students must know, understand, and be able to do as a result of the unit and as a result of each segment of learning in the unit, the chances of alignment among goals, instruction, and assessments is greatly enhanced. Likewise, the likelihood of student success escalates because expectations for students are clear, instruction is focused squarely on expectations, and assessments are crafted to determine each student's proficiency with precisely those expectations. Simple as this sounds, such alignment is uncommon. Using a "backward design" process to ensure a curriculum/instruction/assessment match contributes directly to student achievement and makes "the moment of grading" more transparent—and more honest (Wiggins & McTighe, 1998).

Evidence that contributes to grading should be valid. A grade should communicate clearly and directly what a student knows, understands, and can do in comparison to stated goals at a particular time. No doubt a result of hand-me-down grading practices, teachers subtract points from tests because students forget to write their names, they add points to grades because students complete extra credit projects that are only tangentially related to essential outcomes, they tweak grades because students are nice or difficult, or they lower grades because students don't turn in homework (even though they might make a near perfect grade on the final assessment). A nonnegotiable, meaningful grade is clear communication of student status relative to essential goals. The elimination of "fog-inducing" elements (such as the ones discussed earlier in this chapter) from grades also helps students chart a course to success and maintains student–teacher trust.

Students should be graded on clear criteria, not norms. When students compete against one another in a classroom, it very quickly becomes evident who the winners and losers will be. When they compete against clearly delineated criteria, however, every student has a chance for success. Thus, best-practice grading and differentiation support a "*J* curve," in which all students have the possibility of earning good grades. This is in opposition to a bell-shaped curve, in which only a few students can really succeed (Tomlinson & McTighe, 2006). Consider whether you would prefer a surgeon whose practice is based on a *J* curve or one who literally operates on a bell-shaped curve.

Grade later in a cycle rather than earlier. Schools generally allot a six- to nine-week period for students to develop proficiency with a given set of content goals. This decision suggests that it will take roughly that amount of time for students to achieve those goals, yet we typically begin to grade students on the content early in the marking period and average the early grades with summative grade(s) to yield a final report card grade. The result is that students hear from teachers, "I'm so sorry your grades were low early in the marking period. You made an *A* on your final, but your early grades pulled that down to a *B–*." A summative assessment should be just that—summative. It's of little significance that it took a student the entire marking period to learn the essential knowledge; what should matter most is that he or she is finally able to demonstrate proficiency. If we adhered to the practice of grading later in a cycle rather than earlier, we would encourage persistence (and a growth mind-set) in struggling students who need additional time to learn and in advanced students who may fear tackling work that challenges them will result in lower status.

Report key elements of learner development, but report them separately. It's often difficult to know quite what a grade means. As teachers, we are inclined to report one grade that includes a bit about student achievement, a bit about compliance, and a bit about work habits. The result is that the grade is "mushy." It communicates poorly and does little to further student achievement. There are three elements that teachers in a differentiated classroom need to keep in mind for students and their parents: achievement, habits of mind, and growth. An achievement grade should reflect what a student knows, understands, and can do at a given time relative to stated goals. A grade for habits of mind should indicate the contribution a student makes to his or her own success. Does the student persist in the face of difficulty, ask for help when needed, revise work to improve its quality, set and pursue important academic goals, accept challenges, and look at issues from varied perspectives? A grade focused on student growth should stem from evidence that a student has or has not exhibited measurable progress toward established goals. These three elements should *not* be merged into a single grade. Rather, they should be distinct entities that work together to convey a critical message: People who work effectively will grow, and persistent growth is the key to achieving and exceeding academic goals. This is the core of a growth mind-set. Sadly, it is seldom a vital part of teacher–student, teacher–parent, or parent–student conversations. The ability to keep all three elements in the foreground of teacher, student, and parent thinking would do a great deal to propel student learning in a positive direction. It would also set the stage for continued success in life. Ideally, report cards provide opportunities to grade achievement, habits of mind, and progress. Indeed, some report cards do this, but many do not. (If there is only space for one grade on a report card, it must be the student's achievement grade.) The absence of boxes on a report card, however, should not eliminate the possibility of a teacher monitoring and reporting on all three elements. Teachers who understand the interconnectedness and importance of all three elements in student development can

- Talk with parents and students about all three aspects of student work at the beginning of the year, throughout the year, and at parent–teacher conferences.
- Have students keep ongoing records of all three aspects of their learning.
- Institute parent–student conferences to assess student development in all three areas.
- Add an addendum to a report card in the form of a prose statement or checklist.
- E-mail a three-part report to parents at the end of each marking period.

Teachers who lead for differentiation do many things to shape classroom culture on behalf of student achievement. Publically valuing and ensuring that others understand the value of productive work habits and achievement is an extraordinarily important contribution teachers make to classrooms in which every student is expected to work hard, grow, and succeed.

In an effectively differentiated classroom, support for student achievement does *not* include modifying an achievement grade so it appears that a student has mastered content when he or she has not. Support for student success stems from a growth mind-set teacher; a classroom environment designed and nurtured to build a community in which all students support one another's achievement; a high-quality curriculum that engages students in the difficult work of learning; ongoing assessment that informs the next steps in the learning process (and that incorporates the best practices for assessment and grading noted earlier in this chapter); and instruction that is responsive to students' varied readiness levels, interests, and learning preferences. Under these conditions, grading flows appropriately and naturally.

Concluding Thoughts

We began this book by saying that what lay ahead was aspirational. We'd like to end the book with the same thoughts. Between the two of us, we have a combined teaching experience of about 75 years and have taught preschool, elementary school, high school, undergraduate, masters, and doctoral students.

We understand that teaching is a devilishly difficult profession, made more so by external mandates to achieve the delusional—that is, to ensure that all students reach the same point of mastery of an unwieldy amount of content on the same day, and to demonstrate that mastery under the same conditions.

We know that students' lives have always been complex, and we are keenly aware that the complexity of students' lives is growing exponentially as a result of current events. We know that teachers are responsible for a greater variety of learners with a greater diversity of needs than ever before. We know there is not enough time in the day, not enough days in the week, and not enough weeks in the year to do what teachers need to do. We also know there would be a severe lack of energy to teach additional hours, days, or weeks if they were part of the school calendar.

Nevertheless, we also know that every student that enters every classroom will be enhanced or diminished by the collective attitudes, decisions, and practices of the teachers. We know that every young life that is redeemed by learning is an individual and a collective victory. Likewise, we know that every young life that is scarred by school is an individual and a collective tragedy. We know that contemporary schools and teachers need to develop beyond passive acceptance of what was "good enough" in the past. We know that this can only happen when teachers aspire to do their very best and, in the process, create better ways to ignite the spark of genius found in every human being with the flint of real learning.

It is not our expectation that teachers can read a book, flip a switch, and magically transform their teaching. Rather, we believe that there are teachers who aspire to understand the art and craft of teaching a little better each day, who are willing to take the risk of confronting the power of the work they do, and who are courageous enough to make small and large decisions each day based on benefits to their students. It is to those teachers that we offer the accumulated insights that make up this book.

We know teachers transform lives. We know because we have had the great fortune of being their students. We know because we continue to learn from aspirational teachers—one step at a time, day after year after decade—building careers and lives as they go. This breed of teacher is always more excited than daunted by what lies ahead. We hope you'll join up!

Yes, But . . .

I teach in a four-wall box of drab proportions,
But choose to make it a place that feels like home.
I see too many students to know them as they need to be known,
But refuse to let that render them faceless in my mind.
I am overcome with the transmission of a canon I can scarcely recall myself,
But will not represent learning as a burden to the young.
I suffer from a poverty of time,
And so will use what I have to best advantage those I teach.
I am an echo of the way school has been since forever,
But will not agree to perpetuate the echo another generation.
I am told I am as good a teacher as the test scores I generate,
But will not allow my students to see themselves as data.
I work in isolation,
And am all the more determined to connect my students with the world.
I am small in the chain of power,
But have the power to change young lives.
There are many reasons to succumb,
And thirty reasons five times a day to succeed.
Most decisions about my job are removed from me.
Except the ones that matter most.

Teacher's Toolkit

Getting to Know Your Students Through Glyphs

Explanation:

Glyphs are symbols or icons that can represent all kinds of information about someone or something. There are many examples available on the Internet that offer other ways to learn something about your students. They can provide another visual representation of the diversity of backgrounds and preferences your students have, and they can set the stage for a discussion about why classmates might not always have the same learning tasks or why they might make different choices when the same opportunities are provided. Glyphs can be easily displayed on a bulletin board.

Example:

Provide each student with a paper cutout in the shape of a person. Then give students the following instructions:

1. If you are a boy, color your jeans blue. If you are a girl, color your jeans red.

2. Design a shirt and color it according to your favorite subject:

   • Reading—yellow

   • Math—green

   • Science—orange

   • Social Studies—brown

3. Color your hair according to your least favorite subject.

4. Include your favorite special class on your shirt:

   • Art—Draw an interesting logo.

   • Music—Draw stripes on your shirt.

   • Physical Education—Draw your favorite sport or physical activity.

5. Design a baseball cap and color it purple if you prefer to work by yourself or color it black if you prefer to work with other people.

6. Draw a triangle on your baseball cap for each of your brothers and sisters. Write their names on each triangle.

7. Color your shoes according to your favorite way to learn:
   - Brown—through your ears (auditory)
   - Blue—through your eyes (visual)
   - Black—through moving or using your hands (kinesthetic)

8. Design a backpack to hold in your hand. Make the color of your backpack your favorite color. On the outside, write two wishes you have for this class that you would be willing to share with the class. If you have more than two wishes, or you do not yet want to share them with everyone, write in your journal or talk to me about them when you are ready.

Bio-Poem

Explanation:

Students create and display poems that help the teacher learn more about his or her students and help students learn more about one another. Students generally enjoy completing this kind of poem since it is personal and the pattern is easy to follow. The formula allows for differentiation to best fit the student poets.

Example:

Line 1:	First name
Line 2:	Two phrases about who you are
Line 3:	Four words that describe you
Line 4:	Who likes _____, _____, and _____
Line 5:	Who believes _____
Line 6:	Who wants to be _____
Line 7:	Who worries about _____ and _____
Line 8:	Who has _____, _____, and _____
Line 9:	Who says, "_____"
Line 10:	Last name

Sherrie

14-year-old female
Who has brown hair and green eyes
Who is short, funny, practical, sometimes scared
Who likes to be around my friends, watch TV, and listen to music
Who believes people should be nice to one another
Who wants to be a social worker
Who worries about my little brother and my mom
Who has a great smile, a good heart, and sometimes a forgetful brain
Who says, "Are you kidding me?"

Lamar

Student Profile Cards

Explanation:

Student profile cards help maintain easy-to-access records about students as learners. It's handy to use index cards of different colors for each class period. The front of the card has the name of a student, and the back can be designed to hold whatever information might be useful to plan instruction and assign students to working groups. In the example below, the following information is included:

- place to mark the student's approximate reading level (upper left)
- a checklist of potential learning preferences (lower left)
- a place to jot student interests (center)
- an indicator of the student's affiliation with school (upper right)
- a place to note any identifications for school services (lower right)

Abbreviations are:

- Q/N (Does the student work best with quiet or noise?)
- V/A/K (Does the student gravitate toward visual, auditory, or kinesthetic approaches to learning?)
- G/S (Is the student more of a "groupie" or a "soloist"—in other words, does the student prefer to work with peers or independently?)
- A/P/C (Does the student have particular strengths in analytical, practical, or creative approaches to learning?)
- P/W (Is the student generally a part-to-whole or a whole-to-part learner?)

Example:

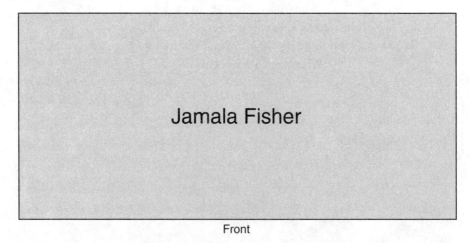

Front

Rdg Level   Sch. Affil.
+321 – 123-   +   –

                        Interests
                         Soccer
LP   Mysteries
Q/N   Video Games
V/A/K
G/S
A/P/C   S/P
P/W   ELL

                          Back

Design Your Own Postcard

Explanation:

Students design a postcard that reveals something about them and what they value. Students can cut out and use pictures from magazines, photographs from home, or images from the Internet. They should focus on finding visuals that tell others about who they are as people.

Example:

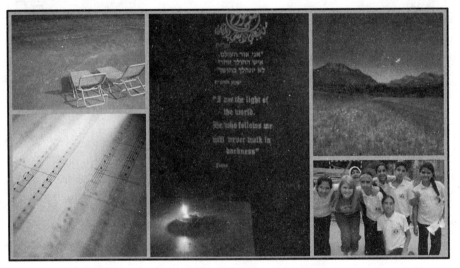

Front

On the reverse side of your postcard, describe the significance of each of your depictions. Explain why you chose each image/word.	List Personal Info: Name Period Parent/Guardian Phone(s) E-mail(s)

Back

Created by Kristina Doubet. Adapted with permission.

Ideas for Building Community

Explanation:

Building a community of learners is important to support student learning and can be created by teachers who intentionally work toward that goal. In essence, everything a teacher does in the classroom can either support or break down a classroom community. The following examples can help build community.

Example:

"I Wonder Who" Game

Have several different-colored squares of construction paper in a small bag for each student. For example, each student might have one square of red, blue, green, and yellow. Have students stand in a circle with their bags, and tell them you are going to ask questions that they will answer with their colored squares. Students should hold up the color that matches their preference (and "answers" the question) and then look around to see how they are the same or different from their classmates. Explain that the questions you will ask do not have any "right" answers, but the responses will help everyone understand what each student likes and doesn't like. Use the questions listed below, or use original questions students would enjoy.

I wonder whose favorite food is . . .
    hamburgers—choose blue
    hot dogs—choose red
    pizza—choose green
    macaroni and cheese—choose yellow

I wonder whose favorite sport is . . .
    soccer—choose blue
    running—choose red
    swimming—choose green
    gymnastics—choose yellow

I wonder whose favorite game is . . .
    a video game—choose blue
    checkers—choose red
    cards—choose green
    Candyland—choose yellow

Line 'Em Up

Explanation:

This is a variation on the "I Wonder Who" game that also requires little preparation and can be adapted for any classroom. Ask students to line up in order from *novice* to *expert* to share how they see themselves at performing various tasks. Explain to students that you will mention a task and they should decide where they see themselves in relation to their classmates. They should then line up and note where their classmates stand and how they see themselves at that task. It's a good idea to join in this activity and demonstrate that you also have strengths and weaknesses (and need to stand in different places), depending on the task. Here are a few examples to get you started.

Example:

- Artistic skills—painting, sculpting, cartooning
- Mechanical skills—building things, fixing things
- Literary skills—writing stories, writing poems, keeping a journal/diary
- Debating skills—persuading someone else of your point of view
- Financial skills—saving money, keeping to a budget

Follow-up Questions:

- Did everyone have a chance to be on the "expert" side of the line?
- Did everyone have a chance to be on the "novice" side of the line?
- Did you learn new things about one another?

Puzzle Pieces

Explanation:

Students work with one another to put together a puzzle that represents something important about an effective class or that represents something they share in common. A teacher might also use puzzle pieces that have students' names written on them along with qualities they believe add to the make-up of the classroom. The purpose of this task is to use puzzle pieces as another way to help build community in the classroom by showing students how they all fit together to make the classroom work. This activity could be used as an ice-breaker for students to meet their classmates since they have to match their puzzle piece with another classmate's. Puzzle pieces can be drawn and cut out of poster board and then randomly given to students to complete the task. A follow-up discussion might ask students how the classroom resembles a puzzle. What is the significance of having individual pieces that fit together to form a cohesive whole?

Example:

Highlighting Students

Explanation:

In an effort to make all students in a classroom feel special, many teachers highlight students so they have an opportunity to "shine" and "share" something about themselves with the rest of the class. Students can bring in photos from home or create drawings of information they wish to share. It is also possible to highlight pairs of students if they would prefer to work with someone else.

Example:

King or Queen for the Day (or Week)
(for younger students)

My name is _____, and I am King/Queen for the Day.

I live in _____ with _____. I have _____ brothers and sisters. Their names are _____. I have _____ pets. They are _____ and their names are _____. My favorite thing to do is _____. I like school when _____.

My name is Michael, and I am King for the Day.

I live in a house with my mom, my dad, and my sisters. I have two sisters.

Their names are Stephanie and Lucy. I have three pets. They are dogs and

their names are Roger, Whitman, and Jacks. My favorite thing to do is play

outside. I like school when we play interesting games.

(**Note:** The teacher can record any information that the student is not yet able to write or draw.)

A Classroom Newsletter
(for older students)

Send home (or post on the school's website) a classroom newsletter that highlights individuals or groups of students in a regular column titled "I Bet You Didn't Know." Students have the opportunity to share something about themselves in terms of their interests, hobbies, experiences, or dreams.

Learning Centers

Explanation:

Students can be assigned to various centers with great flexibility. There may be some centers that everyone attends, such as Meet with the Teacher, and others where only certain students attend, such as Listening Center. Some days, students are assigned to a specific center, and on other days, they can choose to attend a center based on a number of slots available (e.g., Computer Center might only have four slots because of a limited number of computers). Student preferences should be factored into the choices they are offered. In addition, tasks should be engaging and appropriately leveled so work at the centers spurs student growth.

The example schedule below is a convenient way for teachers to keep track of student work and in which centers each student has already worked. The Learning Center table is a great way for students to keep track of their own work.

Example:

Task	Monday	Tuesday	Wednesday	Thursday	Friday
Writing Center	Luis Michael Carla Michelle G.	Alexa Ashley Aaron Brian	Brandon Fran Keisha Nico	Michelle T. Nicholas Angie Miguel	George Jose Anna Matthew Cameron
Computer Center	Jose David Fran	Michelle T. Angie Alexa Matthew	Miguel Brian Daisy Ashley	Nico Brandon George Michael	Carla Nicholas Luis Michelle G.
Book Nook	Brian Aaron Daisy Michelle T.	Keisha Matthew Carla Michelle G.	Michael David Hope	Jose Anna Cameron Alexa	Fran Miguel Angie
Spelling Center	Ashley Brandon Anna Matthew	George David Luis Nico	Cameron Michelle G. Jose Angie	Carla Hope Keisha Daisy	Alexa Aaron
Listening Center	Alexa Keisha	Hope Cameron	Luis Nicholas	Aaron Fran	Michelle T. Brian Ashley

Task	Monday	Tuesday	Wednesday	Thursday	Friday
Word Study	George Nico	Nicholas Miguel	Anna Matthew	Luis Brian	Hope Brandon Daisy David
Meet with the Teacher	Nicholas Angie Miguel Hope Cameron	Jose Brandon Anna Daisy Fran	Aaron Alexa George Michelle T. Carla	Matthew Luis David Ashley Michelle G.	Nico Michael Brian Keisha

Name _____ Month _____

Learning Centers

	Center Activity	Self-Assessment	Teacher Assessment
✔	Creative Cubing Center		
	We've Been Framed		
	Creative Writing Center		
	Don't Forget Your Hat!		
	Math Center		
	Additional activities:		
	Independent project if done early:		

Developed by Debbie Field, 4th grade teacher, New Castle Elementary School, Virginia Beach, Virginia. Used with permission.

Task Cards

Explanation:

Task cards are very useful to remind students of the instructions for completing work. They can be handwritten with heavy markers or printed on index cards, sturdy paper, cardstock, or poster board. Task cards can be placed at learning centers where students can easily check to make sure they know what to do, understand the rules of the center, and know where to put their work when they are finished. Task cards can also be used for small-group work or outlining roles a student might assume while working in a group.

Example:

5th Grade Math RAFT Assignment: Parts of a Whole

- **Group A: Your goal is to communicate that fractions represent parts of whole.**

  - You are to write a children's book similar to Fraction Fun using both text and illustrations. Brainstorm some ideas together. Do not use the same fraction over and over again, and keep in mind that each fraction is speaking to the whole it is a part of. You will be asked to share your books with the other groups.

    - Materials: paper, pencil, crayons, colored pencils

- **Group B: Your goal is to communicate that equivalent fractions are equal and can be expressed by using different numerators and denominators.**

  - You are to fill out the invitation, keeping in mind that you are a fraction inviting one or more of your equivalents to the ball. Brainstorm some possible fractions and their equivalents with your group. Try to be creative and use as many equivalents as possible when thinking about where and when the ball will be held. Use the fraction tiles if you need ideas. Your mask should be colored to represent the equivalent you are inviting, and no two invitations and masks should be exactly the same. Then write a letter about why certain fractions were invited and why others were not. You will be asked to share your final product with the other groups.

    - Materials: invitation template, mask, pencil, crayons, colored pencils, fraction tiles.

Developed by Michelle Krolikowski, Gifted Resource Teacher, New Castle Elementary School, Virginia Beach, Virginia. Used with permission.

- **Group C: Your goal is to communicate that fractions and decimals are related and represent parts of wholes. There is a decimal representation for each fraction.**

  - You will quickly convert several fractions into their decimal forms. You may use a calculator or your dry erase boards. Choose your fraction and fill out the wanted poster, keeping in mind that you are the fraction and you are describing your decimal number. Your illustration should show your fraction, but your writing should describe your decimal. You will be asked to share these with the other groups.
    - Materials: calculators, dry erase boards and markers, wanted poster template, pencil, crayons, colored pencils

- **Group D: Your goal is to communicate that fractioins can be represented as a decimal and a percent.**

  - You will begin by converting several fractions to decimals and then to percents. Use a calculator or your erase board. Choose the fraction and dress your paper people as a visual representation of the conversions. Then write a short story on notebook paper about the changing wardrobe. You will be asked to share your work with the other groups.
    - Materials: calculators, dry erase boards and markers, notebook paper, paper person templates, crayons, colored pencils

Developed by Michelle Krolikowski, Gifted Resource Teacher, New Castle Elementary School, Virginia Beach, Virginia. Used with permission.

Hint Cards

Explanation:

Hint cards are designed to assist students who may become "stuck" as they complete an assignment. Teachers might record reminders or tips on task cards or worksheets and keep them organized in folders that are prominently displayed in the classroom. Hint cards provide students with a self-help method to handle questions they have about an assignment. They also help students return to the task without having to ask the teacher for help.

Example:

Developed by Sherri Kulpa, Kirkwood, Colorado. Used with permission.

Other hint examples:

Activity Pages with editorial comments added (not answers, but tips on how to proceed or reminders about where answers might be located)

Writing frames for particular formats (friendly letters, book reviews, letters to the editor, persuasive essays, informational pieces, etc.)

Product exemplars (brochures, posters, web pages, book trailers, PowerPoint or other presentation tips, model instructions, demonstration guidelines, etc.)

Clinics

Explanation:

Clinics are help sessions that are offered periodically or routinely throughout a week or unit of study when assistance is needed. Generally, clinic schedules are posted and students sign up if they need to attend. A teacher can meet with students individually or in small groups to answer questions or offer specific assistance so students can proceed with an assignment or project.

Example:

Clinics can be effective activities when

- Students have been working on a longer writing assignment and need help with organization and ideas.
- Students have been working on independent projects and need to go over their progress and make sure they are on track to meet the deadline.
- Students have been working on a homework assignment in class and are unsure if they are completing the assignment correctly.

Anchor Activities

Explanation:

Anchor activities are tasks that can be completed by students independently. Access to these activities ensures that students always have productive work options, especially when they need to start and stop work at different times or when they finish an assignment ahead of others. Anchor activities are appropriate at all grade levels and limit the number of times that students rush to the teacher and announce, "I'm finished, now what?" Change the anchor options periodically so student interest and engagement remain high and so students continually make new connections to relevant content.

Example:

"I Can" Poster
(for lower elementary students)

Anchor Activity Options
(for upper elementary / middle school students)

- Work on your book report selection (read quietly until time is called). If you have already finished your book, then work on your review (consult the hint box for guidelines).
- Complete one of the three journal prompts provided.
- Select a Learning Interest packet from the anchor option file box.
- Select at least one area of test prep practice you believe you need to review.
- Work on your Orbital or Independent Project.

Anchor Activity Options
(for secondary students)

- Journals or learning logs
- "Project extensions"
- Independent reading
- Lab work
- Related course readings with questions or extension activities
- Test prep or practice test reviews for ACT or SAT
- Project interests
- Learning packets
- Independent studies
- Computer skills
- WebQuests or telecollaborative projects

Orbitals

Explanation:

An orbital study focuses on a topic of student interest related to some facet of the curriculum. They are called orbitals because they are extensions of a unit of study on a specific topic that students wish to learn more about. Students may work on orbitals for varied lengths of time, depending on the nature of the topic and the student's ability to sustain independent work. Teachers help students develop clear questions for study, a plan for research, a method of presentation, and criteria to measure quality. Successfully completing an orbital includes keeping a log of time spent on the study, resources used, ideas developed, and skills gained.

Teachers may have a standard planning form that can assist students as they organize their ideas for completing an orbital. For example, the form could require students to describe the topic they wish to investigate, list questions they believe will be important for them to pursue, identify resources they think can be helpful, brainstorm methods to share their research with an audience, and create a timeline for completing the work.

Example:

After a unit about the Holocaust, Maggie decides to research the genocide in Darfur to learn more about the conflict and compare the two historical events. She develops three questions to guide her research:

- What were contributing factors that caused the violence in Darfur?
- What is being done to help those who have been affected by the conflict?
- In what ways is the Darfur conflict similar to or different from the Holocaust?

Maggie begins by looking up information posted online at the United States Holocaust Memorial Museum's website. In addition, she wants to interview a local resident who has visited Darfur and is an advocate for making the world aware of that region's atrocities. Her timeline for completing this work is two weeks. The teacher has agreed that Maggie's orbital will serve as an anchor activity; anytime such activities are available to students, Maggie may work on her project in class. To ensure that the project is on track, the teacher schedules a "check in" conference with Maggie before the end of the first week.

Maggie will ultimately develop a podcast that will be posted on her school's website and made available to the larger community, including the student body and visitors to the school. This project provides Maggie with an opportunity to pursue an area of personal interest, develop her research and presentation skills, utilize technology tools, and educate others.

Request for Additional Time on a Project

Explanation:

When students feel they have a legitimate need for more time to complete a project, they can make and submit a formal request. Completing the form causes students to reflect on their work habits, planning and organizational skills, and personal goals. In addition, completing the form allows students at all levels another opportunity to take responsibility for their learning. When an extension of time is granted, it should provide an opportunity to generate a product that is at a very high level of quality. An extension is not intended to help students "squeak by."

Example:

Dear _____,

    Yikes! I ran out of time to complete my _____.

I have
(*Check all that apply*)

      ❐ Developed my questions.
      ❐ Found my resources.
      ❐ Found answers to my questions.
      ❐ Made my product.
      ❐ Other: _____.

I still need to
(*Check all that apply*)

      ❐ Make my product.
      ❐ Prepare my presentation.
      ❐ Other: _____.

    I believe my project will be much better if I have extra time because _____
_____.
I would like to request that my new deadline be changed to _____
_____.

Your student,

Teacher's decision: _____

Additional comments:

References

Allington, R. (1994). The schools we have, the schools we need. *The Reading Teacher, 48*(1), 14–29.

Aronson, J., Fried, C., & Good, C. (2002). Reducing the effects of stereotype threat on African American college students by shaping theories of intelligence. *Journal of Experimental Social Psychology, 38*(2), 113–125.

Beane, J. (2005). *A reason to teach: Creating classrooms of dignity and hope.* Portsmouth, NH: Heinemann.

Bondy, E., & Ross, D. (2008). The teacher as warm demander. *Educational Leadership, 66*(1), 54–58.

Brighton, C. M., Hertberg, H. L., Moon, T. R., Tomlinson, C. A., & Callahan, C. M. (2005). *The feasibility of high-end learning in a diverse middle school.* Storrs, CT: National Research Center on the Gifted and Talented.

Carbonaro, W., & Gamoran, A. (2002). The production of achievement inequality in high school English. *American Educational Research Journal, 39*(4), 801–827.

Cohen, E. (1994). *Designing groupwork: Strategies for the heterogeneous classroom* (2nd ed.). New York: Teachers College Press.

Collins, M., & Amabile, T. (1999). Motivation and creativity. In R. J. Sternberg (Ed.), *Handbook of creativity* (pp. 297–312). New York: Cambridge University Press.

Cone, J. (2003). The construction of low achievement: A study of one detracked senior English class. *Harvard Education Letter, 19*(3), 4–5.

Cookson, P. (2009). What would Socrates say? *Educational Leadership, 67*(1), 10–12.

Craig, S. (2008). *Reaching and teaching children who hurt: Strategies for your classroom.* Baltimore: Paul H. Brookes.

Csikszentmihalyi, M. (1990). *Flow: The psychology of optimal experience.* New York: HarperCollins.

Cummings, C. (2000). *Winning strategies for classroom management.* Alexandria, VA: ASCD.

Darling-Hammond, L. (2009). *The flat world and education: How America's commitment to equity will determine our future.* New York: Teachers College Press.

Delpit, L. (1995). *Other people's children: Cultural conflict in the classroom.* New York: The New Press.

DuFour, R., & Eaker, R. (1998). *Professional learning communities at work: Best practices for enhancing student achievement.* Bloomington, IN: Solution Tree.

Dunn, R., & Dunn, K. (1992). *Teaching elementary students through their individual learning styles: Practical approaches for grades 3–6.* Boston: Allyn & Bacon.

Dunn, R., & Dunn, K. (1993). *Teaching secondary students through their individual learning styles: Practical approaches for grades 7–12.* Boston: Allyn & Bacon.

Dweck, C. (2000). *Self theories: Their role in motivation, personality, and development.* Philadelphia, PA: Psychology Press.

Dweck, C. (2006). *Mindset: The new psychology of success.* New York: Random House.

Earl, L. (2003). *Assessment as learning: Using classroom assessment to maximize student learning.* Thousand Oaks, CA: Corwin Press.

Educational Research Service. (1993). *Academic challenge for the children of poverty.* Arlington, VA: Author.

Erickson, H. L. (2006). *Concept-based curriculum and instruction for the thinking classroom.* Thousand Oaks, CA: Corwin Press.

Finnian, C., & Swanson, J. (2000). *Accelerating the learning of all students: Cultivating culture change in schools, classrooms, and individuals.* Boulder, CO: Westview.

Fullan, M. (2001a). *Leading in a culture of change.* San Francisco: Jossey-Bass.

Fullan, M. (2001b). *The new meaning of educational change* (3rd ed.). New York: Teachers College Press.

Fullan, M. (2007). *The new meaning of educational change* (4th ed.). New York: Teachers College Press.

Gamoran, A., Nystrand, M., Berends, M., & LePore, P. (1995). An organizational analysis of the effects of ability grouping. *American Educational Research Journal, 32*(4), 687–715.

Gardner, H. (1985). *Frames of mind: The theory of multiple intelligences.* New York: BasicBooks.

Gardner, J. (1961). *Excellence: Can we be equal and excellent too?* New York: Harper & Row.

Gilligan, C. (1982). *In a different voice: Psychological theory and women's development.* Cambridge, MA: Harvard University Press.

Good, C., Aronson, J., & Inzlicht, M. (2003). Improving adolescents' standardized test performance: An intervention to reduce the effects of stereotype threat. *Applied Developmental Psychology, 24,* 645–662.

Greene, M. (2000). *Releasing the imagination: Essays on education, the arts, and social change.* San Francisco: Jossey-Bass.

Greene, R. (2008). *Lost at school: Why our kids with behavioral challenges are falling through the cracks and how we can help them.* New York: Scribner.

Gregorc, A. (1979). Learning/teaching styles: Potent forces behind them. *Educational Leadership, 36,* 234–236.

Grigorenko, E., Jarvin, L., & Sternberg, R. (2002). School-based tests of the triarchic theory of intelligence: Three settings, three samples, three syllabi. *Contemporary Educational Psychology, 27*(2), 167–208.

Gurian, M. (2001). *Boys and girls learn differently: A guide for teachers and parents.* San Francisco: Jossey-Bass.

Guskey, T. (2000). Grading policies that work against standards . . . and how to fix them. *NASSP Bulletin, 84*(620), 20–27.

Guskey, T., & Bailey, J. (2001). *Developing grading and reporting systems for student learning.* Thousand Oaks, CA: Corwin Press.

Haberman, M. (1991). The pedagogy of poverty versus good teaching. *Phi Delta Kappan, 73*(4), 290–294.

Heath, S. (1983). *Ways with words: Language, life and work in communities and classrooms.* Cambridge, England: Cambridge University Press.

Hilliard, A. (2003). No mystery: Closing the achievement gap. In T. Perry, A. Hilliard, & C. Steele (Eds.), *Young, gifted, and black: Promoting high achievement among African American students* (pp. 131–165). Boston: Beacon.

Hodges, H. (2001). Overcoming a pedagogy of poverty. In R. W. Cole (Ed.), *More strategies for educating everybody's children* (pp. 1–9). Alexandria, VA: ASCD.

Hopfenberg, W., & Levin, H. (2008). *The accelerated schools resource guide.* San Francisco: Jossey-Bass.

INTASC. (1992) *Model standards for beginning teacher licensing, assessment and development: A resource for state dialogue.* Washington, DC: Interstate New Teacher Assessment and Support Consortium.

Kopp, W. (2001). *One day, all children . . . : The unlikely triumph of Teach for America and what I learned along the way.* New York: Perseus Books.

Lasley, T., Matczynski, T., & Rowley, J. (1997). *Instructional models: Strategies for teaching in a diverse society.* Belmont, CA: Wadsworth.

LePage, P., Darling-Hammond, L., & Akar, H. (2005). Classroom management. In L. Darling-Hammond & J. Bransford (Eds.), *Preparing teachers for a changing world: What teachers should learn and be able to do* (pp. 327–357). San Francisco: Jossey-Bass.

Marx, G. (2000). *Ten trends: Educating children for a profoundly different future.* Arlington, VA: Educational Research Service.

Marzano, R. J. (2000). *Transforming classroom grading.* Alexandria, VA: ASCD.

Marzano, R. J., Marzano, J. S., & Pickering, D. J. (2003). *Classroom management that works: Research-based strategies for every teacher.* Alexandria, VA: ASCD.

Maslow, A. H. (1943). A theory of human motivation. *Psychological Review, 50*(4), 370–396.

National Association for the Education of Young Children. (2001). NAEYC Standards for Early Childhood Preparation: Baccalaureate or Initial Licensure Level. Retrieved November 26, 2009, from http://condor.admin.ccny.cuny.edu/~echilded/naeyc%202001.pdf

National Association for the Education of Young Children. (2009). Developmentally appropriate practice in early childhood programs serving children from birth through age 8: A position statement of the National Association for the Education of Young Children. Retrieved November 26, 2009, from http://www.naeyc.org/files/naeyc/file/positions/PSDAP.pdf

National Association of Secondary School Principals. (2004). *Breaking ranks II: Strategies for leading high school reform.* Reston, VA: Author.

National Association of Secondary School Principals. (2005). NASSP Legislative recommendations for high school reform. Retrieved May 8, 2010, from http://www.principals.org/Portals/0/Content/49743.pdf

National Board for Professional Teaching Standards. (2010). The standards. Retrieved May 8, 2010, from http://www.nbpts.org/the_standards/the_five_core_propositions

National Middle School Association. (2010). This we believe: Essential attributes and characteristics of successful schools. Retrieved November 26, 2009, from www.nmsa.org/AboutNMSA/ThisWeBelieve/The16Characteristics/tabid/1274/Default.aspx

National Research Council. (2000). *How people learn: Brain, mind, experience, and school.* Washington, DC: National Academies Press.

O'Connor, K. (2002). *How to grade for learning: Linking grades to standards* (2nd ed.). Thousand Oaks, CA: Corwin Press.

Olson, K. (2009). *Wounded by school: Recapturing the joy in learning and standing up to old school culture.* New York: Teachers College Press.

Paley, V. G. (1993). *You can't say you can't play.* Cambridge, MA: Harvard University Press.

Reeves, D. (2009). *Leading change in your school: How to conquer myths, build commitment, and get results.* Alexandria, VA: ASCD.

Rothstein-Fisch, C., & Trumbull, E. (2008). *Managing diverse classrooms: How to build on students' cultural strengths.* Alexandria, VA: ASCD.

Schlechty, P. (1997). *Inventing better schools: An action plan for educational reform.* San Francisco: Jossey-Bass.

Sizer, T. (1985). *Horace's Compromise: The dilemma of the American high school.* Boston: Houghton-Mifflin.

Sousa, D. (2001). *How the brain learns* (2nd ed.). Thousand Oaks, CA: Corwin Press.

Sternberg, R. J. (1985). *Beyond IQ: A triarchic theory of human intelligence.* New York: Cambridge University Press.

Sternberg, R., Torff, B., & Grigorenko, E. (1998). Teaching triarchically improves school achievement. *Journal of Educational Psychology, 90*(3), 374–384.

Stronge, J. (2002). *Qualities of effective teachers.* Alexandria, VA: ASCD.

Tannen, D. (1990). *You just don't understand: Women and men in conversation.* New York: Ballantine.

Tomlinson, C. (1999). *The differentiated classroom: Responding to the needs of all learners.* Alexandria, VA: ASCD.

Tomlinson, C. (2001). *How to differentiate instruction in mixed-ability classrooms* (2nd ed.). Alexandria, VA: ASCD.

Tomlinson, C. (2004). *Fulfilling the promise of the differentiated classroom: Strategies and tools for responsive teaching.* Alexandria, VA: ASCD.

Tomlinson, C., Brighton, C., Hertberg, H., Callahan, C., Moon, T., Brimijoin, K., Conover, L., & Reynolds, T. (2003). Differentiating instruction in response to student readiness, interest, and learning profile in academically diverse classrooms: A review of literature. *Journal for the Education of the Gifted, 27*(2/3), 119–145.

Tomlinson, C., Brimijoin, K., & Narvaez, L. (2008). *The differentiated school: Making revolutionary changes in teaching and learning.* Alexandria, VA: ASCD.

Tomlinson, C., & McTighe, J. (2006). *Integrating differentiated instruction & understanding by design: Connecting content and kids.* Alexandria, VA: ASCD.

Tomlinson, J., Kaplan, C., Renzulli, S., Purcell, J., Leppien, J., Burns, D., Strickland, C. A., & Imbeau, M. (2009). *The parallel curriculum: A design to develop learner potential and challenge advanced learners* (2nd ed.). Thousand Oaks, CA: Corwin Press.

Tompkins, J. (1996). *A life in school: What the teacher learned.* New York: Perseus Books.

Villa, R., & Thousand, J. (2005). *Creating an inclusive school* (2nd ed.). Alexandria, VA: ASCD.

Vygotsky, L. S. (1978). *Mind in society.* Cambridge, MA: Harvard University Press.

Vygotsky, L. S. (1986). *Thought and language.* Cambridge, MA: MIT Press.

Wagner, T. (2008). *The global achievement gap: Why even the best schools don't teach the new survival skills our students need, and what we can do about it.* New York: BasicBooks.

Ware, F. (2006). Warm demander pedagogy: Culturally responsive teaching that supports a culture of achievement for African American students. *Urban Education, 41*(4), 427–456.

Wiggins, G. (1992). Foreword. In R. Villa, J. Thousand, W. Stainback, & S. Stainback (Eds.), *Restructuring for caring and effective education: An administrative guide to creating heterogeneous schools* (pp. xv–xvi). Baltimore, MD: Paul H. Brookes.

Wiggins, G. (1993). *Assessing student performance.* San Francisco: Jossey-Bass.

Wiggins, G., & McTighe, J. (1998). *Understanding by design.* Alexandria, VA: ASCD.

Wiggins, G., & McTighe, J. (2005). *Understanding by design* (2nd ed.). Alexandria, VA: ASCD.

Wolfe, P. (2010). *Brain matters: Translating research into classroom practice* (2nd ed.). Alexandria, VA: ASCD.

Zhao, Y. (2009). *Catching up or leading the way: American education in the age of globalization.* Alexandria, VA: ASCD.

Index

The letter *f* following a page number denotes a figure.

About the Authors

Carol Ann Tomlinson

Carol Ann Tomlinson began her career in education as a public school teacher, ultimately spending 21 years as a classroom teacher and in various administrative roles. During that time, she taught preschool, middle school, and high school students in the content areas of English/language arts, history, and German. She also served as director of programs for advanced and struggling learners and as a community relations coordinator. While a teacher in the Fauquier County (Virginia) public schools, she received recognition as Outstanding Teacher at Warrenton Junior High School, Jaycees Outstanding Young Educator, American Legion Outstanding Educator, and the Soroptimist Distinguished Women in Education Award. She was named Virginia's Teacher of the Year in 1974.

Currently the William Clay Parrish, Jr. Professor and Chair of Educational Leadership, Foundations, and Policy at the University of Virginia's Curry School of Education, where she is also Co-Director of the University's Institutes on Academic Diversity, Tomlinson works with both graduate and undergraduate students, particularly in the areas of curriculum and differentiated instruction. She was named Outstanding Professor at Curry in 2004 and received an All-University Teaching Award in 2008.

Tomlinson, along with several colleagues, has researched differentiation in a variety of contexts. Among them are preservice teachers' understanding of and ability to address student differences; the nature of the change process in schools that implement differentiation; achievement impacts of differentiation in middle school, elementary, and high school settings; and profiles of teachers whose classroom practice enhances success of students from low-economic and/or cultural minority groups.

Her more than 250 books, book chapters, articles, and other educational materials include (for ASCD): *How to Differentiate Instruction in Mixed-Ability Classrooms* (2nd edition), *The Differentiated Classroom: Responding to the Needs of All Learners, Fulfilling the Promise of the Differentiated Classroom: Strategies and Tools for Responsive Teaching, Integrating Differentiated Instruction & Understanding by Design: Connecting Content and Kids* (with Jay McTighe), and *The Differentiated School: Making Revolutionary Changes in Teaching and Learning* (with Kay Brimijoin and Lane Narvaez).

She works regularly throughout the United States and internationally with educators who seek to create classrooms that are more effective with academically diverse student populations. She can be reached at the University of Virginia's Curry School of Education, P.O. Box 400277, Charlottesville, VA 22904, or by e-mail at cat3y@virginia.edu.

Marcia B. Imbeau

Marcia B. Imbeau is an associate professor in the Department of Curriculum and Instruction at the University of Arkansas at Fayetteville, where she teaches graduate courses in childhood education and gifted education. She is actively involved in university and public school partnerships, working regularly with her interns and their mentor teachers as a university liaison and teaching courses in curriculum development, differentiation, classroom management, and action research. She was awarded the College of Education and Health Professions' Outstanding Teaching Award in 2000 and 2003.

Imbeau's professional experience includes teaching in a general education classroom, teaching in programs for students identified as gifted, and coordinating university-based enrichment programs for advanced learners. She has served as a board member and member of the executive committee of the National Association for Gifted Children and of the Council for Exceptional Children's TAG division. She has also served as the president of Arkansans for Gifted and Talented Education, a state organization that supports appropriate services for all students.

Among her publications are *The Parallel Curriculum: A Design to Develop Learner Potential and Challenge Advanced Learners* (2nd Edition) (with Carol Tomlinson, Sandy Kaplan, Joseph Renzulli, Jeanne Purcell, Jann Leppien, Deborah Burns, and Cindy Strickland); a book chapter, "Designing a Professional Development Program," for *Designing Services and Programs for High-Ability Learners: A Guidebook for Gifted Education* edited by J. H. Purcell and R. D. Eckert; and *How to Use Differentiated Instruction with Students with Developmental Disabilities in the General Education Classroom* (with Barbara Gartin, Nikki Murdick, and Darlene Perner).

Imbeau has been a regular presenter at ASCD conferences and institutes and, as a member of the ASCD Differentiated Instruction Cadre, works regularly with schools and districts to help teachers and leaders implement differentiation as a vehicle for achieving success for all learners. She can be reached at the University of Arkansas, G05 Stone House, Department of Curriculum and Instruction, Fayetteville, AR 72701, or by e-mail at mimbeau@uark.edu.

Related ASCD Resources

At the time of publication, the following ASCD resources were available (ASCD stock numbers appear in parentheses). For up-to-date information about ASCD resources, go to www.ascd.org. You can search the complete archives of *Educational Leadership* at http://www.ascd.org/el.

ASCD EDge Group

Exchange ideas and connect with other educators interested in differentiated instruction on the social networking site ASCD EDge™ at http://ascdedge.ascd.org/

Print Products

Differentiated Literacy Coaching: Scaffolding for Student and Teacher Success by Mary Catherine Moran (#107053)

The Differentiated School: Making Revolutionary Changes in Teaching and Learning by Carol Ann Tomlinson, Kay Brimijoin, and Lane Narvaez (#105005)

Exploring Differentiated Instruction by Cindy Strickland (#109039)

Fulfilling the Promise of the Differentiated Classroom: Strategies and Tools for Responsive Teaching by Carol Ann Tomlinson (#103107)

How to Differentiate Instruction in Mixed-Ability Classrooms (2nd edition) by Carol Ann Tomlinson (#101043)

Leadership for Differentiating Schools and Classrooms by Carol Ann Tomlinson and Susan Demirsky Allan (#100216)

Videos

At Work in the Differentiated Classroom (#601071)

A Visit to a School Moving Toward Differentiation (#607133)

Leadership for Differentiating Instruction (#607038)

THE WHOLE CHILD The Whole Child Initiative helps schools and communities create learning environments that allow students to be healthy, safe, engaged, supported, and challenged. To learn more about other books and resources that relate to the whole child, visit www.wholechildeducation.org.

For more information: send e-mail to member@ascd.org; call 1-800-933-2723 or 703-578-9600, press 2; send a fax to 703-575-5400; or write to Information Services, ASCD, 1703 N. Beauregard St., Alexandria, VA 22311-1714 USA.